THE
BUCKET LIST
ACTIVITY BOOK
for Couples

Deep Questions and Meaningful Activities to Help Plan Your Life's Adventures

Dr. Carol Morgan

Illustrations by Adam Howling

ROCKRIDGE PRESS

To my husband, Joe.
I hope this book helps other couples
stay as happy and in love as we are.
I love you madly.

Contents

Introduction

WELCOME TO *The Bucket List Activity Book for Couples*! Designed for both new and long-standing couples, this book contains 120 prompts and activities to help you assemble an ultimate bucket list of things you want to try as a couple. Each activity will inspire you to cultivate your connection and increase feelings of intimacy. The pages ahead will give you prompts to encourage you to discuss mutual goals and dreams, to be creative, and to have lots of fun!

Spending time together doing meaningful, enjoyable things can build intimacy and create a stronger bond between the two of you—and building a bucket list can increase that bond even more. Many of us think of bucket lists as lists of individual goals and dreams, but it's just as important to create one for your relationship. It will help motivate you to keep trying new things and to not put off fun until some faraway future when you have "more time."

I am a dating and relationship coach, professor, speaker, writer, and motivational expert who regularly appears on the TV show *Living Dayton*. I have been interested in romantic relationships for most of my life. This fascination led me to earn my PhD in gender and interpersonal communication and later become a professor at Wright State University, where I have been since 1999.

As I worked with couples throughout my career, I discovered that many people get too comfortable in their relationships. In fact, some stop having fun with each other altogether. But this isn't healthy—it could lead to complacency, which in turn could lead to drifting apart from your partner. Relationships without the joy of building connections start to wither and die. Just as a plant needs watering and tending to, so does a relationship. It's so important to keep the spark alive—and that's what this book will help you actively do!

How to Use This Book

This book offers meaningful prompts for deep conversations and fun activities that will help you create more mutual vulnerability, sharing, and openness in your relationship. They are not only designed to inspire and help you have fun—each activity will also help you create a unique personal bucket list item as a couple.

Part 1 consists of 120 prompts that are structured to facilitate fun and meaningful interaction between the two of you. Each of these prompts and activities can help you develop or strengthen one or more of the primary dimensions of intimacy in a couple: emotional, intellectual, experiential, and physical. You will find each prompt labeled with the icons representing these four dimensions of intimacy:

 Emotional: This is when people feel safe sharing their feelings with each other—both positive and negative ones. Emotional intimacy helps you feel deep emotions and connection toward your partner.

 Intellectual: This is when people feel comfortable sharing their ideas and opinions about the world. You feel like you have a meaningful intellectual connection to your partner.

 Experiential: This is when people bond with each other by doing activities together. By doing so, they strengthen their connection through teamwork and cooperation.

 Physical: This is when people use touch to foster closeness. When we ponder this type of intimacy, we may think of sex, but physical intimacy can be strengthened by a wide range of behavior that incorporates all kinds of touch and physical closeness to build connection between two people.

You don't have to complete the prompts and activities in order, but eventually each one will lead to an item to add to your couple's bucket list. Not only will the prompts help you build up the four dimensions of intimacy, but they will also help you come up with personalized bucket list items through reflection questions at the end of each activity. Part 2 consists of the Master Bucket List and Tracker where you can write down each item and keep track of your progress.

The book includes many spaces to write, draw, and otherwise engage in prompts. If you're using an e-book reader, you can write down your prompts on a separate sheet of paper instead.

When you finish this book, you will have a complete list of bucket list items that you can check off as you fulfill each one. While engaging with each other through these prompts is a great first step toward strengthening your relationship, following through on the items you've added to your bucket list is another important step for you as a couple, to help bond you even more deeply as these mutual goals and experiences are accomplished together.

PART 1

DISCOVERING OUR BUCKET LIST

In this part, you will find 120 prompts that will help you engage meaningfully with your partner. The prompts may involve writing, a fun activity or game, or just talking. All types of prompts will ultimately serve as inspiration for you to work as a team and create more intimacy between the two of you—whether it is emotional, intellectual, experiential, and/or physical. Finally, these prompts also help you create your own personalized bucket list so that you can continue to build intimacy and explore fun and unique experiences in your lives together.

After each prompt, a Reflect and Plan section will guide you and your partner in further discussion and help you brainstorm ideas for your bucket list.

It's often difficult for couples to come up with their own unique things to talk about because they are so used to discussing everyday events and details. But these prompts will help you dig deep intellectually and emotionally—and have fun.

BREAK IT DOWN

Goals, dreams, or bucket list ideas can feel too big or overwhelming at times, and you may not know where or how to start. These things can be easier to achieve if you break them down into smaller steps. For example, if your goal is "write a book," then the smaller steps or goals could be "write a book proposal" and "write three pages a day no matter what."

Write down one goal, then try to break it down. You may even want to try easier and harder variations of your goal. For example, related to acting, you may include: acting in a local play, getting booked for a television commercial, and being an extra in a movie.

PARTNER A

1. _____
2. _____
3. _____

PARTNER B

1. _____
2. _____
3. _____

Reflect and Plan: Try to do this for all your bucket list items, and as you do this, you may find that you have even more ideas!

Bucket List Items: _____

_____

_____

OUT ABOUT TOWN

Sometimes you can live in one place for years and never visit any of the places your city or town is known for. This is your opportunity to be a tourist in your town. Do a little research with your partner on places you can visit in your town. Is there a haunted house? What is the tallest point in your city? What is the oldest business? Did any famous people live in your town? Maybe there are places you just want to show your partner because they hold special meaning for you. Create a combined list of places that you want to visit together.

PLACES TO VISIT

1. _____

2. _____

3. _____

4. _____

5. _____

6. _____

7. _____

8. _____

9. _____

10. _____

Reflect and Plan: Now that you have a list, plan an itinerary for your next date. Don't forget to add something special to your tour. Maybe you can picnic at the tallest location in your town, hold hands, and watch the sunset. Does this date make it to your bucket list?

Bucket List Items: _____

_____

_____

DREAM TEAM

If you were to have a superpower, what would it be? How would you help the world with this power?

On separate sheets of paper, draw your partner as a superhero. Don't worry—you don't have to be a skilled artist to do this. If you want, just talk about them. Just try to make it as detailed as you can, from hair color to their accessories. Give your superheroes creative names.

After you create the superheroes, talk about how they could work in a storyline together. Who would be the villain(s) and how would you fight them off as a team? Really think about how these superheroes would work well together as you brainstorm and write.

Supplies Needed: Paper; colored pencils, markers, or crayons

Plot: _____

_____

_____

_____

_____

_____

Villain(s): _____

_____

_____

_____

_____

_____

Climax: _____

_____

_____

_____

_____

_____

Ending: _____

_____

_____

_____

_____

_____

Reflect and Plan: What kinds of things could you do that would require a superhero attitude or bravery? Do you need to wear a costume, or act anonymously, or have a secret identity?

Bucket List Item: _____

_____

_____

DINE IN THE DARK

Though you may think there's no way to make dining at home feel new or different, there's a way to add a new dimension that you may not have considered: Turn off the lights.

Cook a favorite romantic dinner, then turn off all the lights in the house so it's as dark as possible. If your house doesn't get very dark, try using blindfolds so you can't see anything. Then sit down to your meal.

Start by trying to feed yourself, and then feed each other. Make sure to use only blunt or plastic utensils or your hands, for safety. (Don't wield a steak knife in the dark!) Between the laughter and fumbling, talk to each about the experience. Does the food taste different in the dark? Can you immediately tell what each piece of food is when you pick it up or taste it? How difficult is it to find your partner's mouth in the dark? It adds a layer of mystery to the meal and engages your senses in a new way.

Supplies Needed: Food, plates, utensils, blindfolds (optional)

Reflect and Plan: What other kinds of regular activities can be made more interesting by changing something about how you do them? Is there anything else you normally do in the light that you'd like to try in the dark?

Bucket List Items: _____

_____

_____

MYSTERY BOX

Each one of you should select an object. Do not show what it is to your partner. Put the objects in a box and sit facing each other with the box in front of you. Take turns asking questions about the objects, but you can ask only yes-or-no questions. Keep asking until you can guess what object your partner chose. The partner to guess correctly first wins.

Supplies Needed: Boxes, selected objects

Keep a record of your experience here, if you'd like. Was it hard or easy to guess what object each partner chose?

_____

_____

_____

_____

_____

_____

Reflect and Plan: Mysteries can be both exciting and scary. How can you create and experience more mystery in your life as a couple?

Bucket List Item: _____

_____

_____

ALIEN FRIENDS

Is there life on other planets? Will the aliens be friend or foe? This is your chance to really talk about the possibilities and get creative about the idea of life beyond what we know.

Take some time to make up your own alien race. What is the name of their planet? How is their life/planet different from ours? Then, on separate sheets of paper, take the time to draw what these aliens would look like.

Supplies Needed: Paper, crayons or markers, pencils

PARTNER A

Planet name: _____

How they communicate: _____

_____

_____

What they eat: _____

_____

_____

What they wear: _____

_____

_____

Technological development: _____

_____

_____

Form of government: _____

_____

_____

PARTNER B

Planet name: _____

How they communicate: _____
_____
_____

What they eat: _____
_____
_____

What they wear: _____
_____
_____

Technological development: _____
_____
_____

Form of government: _____
_____
_____

Reflect and Plan: Think about some fun things you could do together that are related to outer space. This could be anything from going to a planetarium to planning a trip to see a rocket launch at Cape Canaveral. The sky is *not* the limit!

Bucket List Item: _____
_____
_____

FIRST-DATE TRIVIA GAME

You and your partner probably both have strong memories of your very first date. But how similar are the memories?

For this activity, each of you will write down on separate sheets of paper the things you remember most from your first date. It could be the food, the clothes you wore, the conversations you had, or anything else that was important to you.

Then each partner will guess what the other one has on their list. When you get one right, you get one point. Whoever has the most points wins! When you're done guessing, it's nice to just go through the list and see how you each remember the day.

Supplies Needed: Paper, pens or pencils

SCORES

Partner A: _____

Partner B: _____

Reflect and Plan: What was it about your first date that made you want to keep seeing your partner? Do those things still figure into your life today? Is there anything you'd change about that date?

Bucket List Items: _____

_____

_____

UNCONVENTIONAL

Choose a random object in your home, or something in front of you if you're not at home. Brainstorm how this item can be used in ways it is not being used now. Try to think outside the box, or, using caution, play around with it to come up with more ideas.

PARTNER A
Object: _____

New use: _____

_____

PARTNER B
Object: _____

New use: _____

_____

Reflect and Plan: Many people do things in conventional ways. They follow routines and societal norms. What can you do that would be fun and exciting that would be considered by most to be unconventional?

Bucket List Item: _____

_____

_____

NEW BEGINNINGS

Each of you will come up with five new ideas you want to try to improve your relationship. These can be simple, such as waking up 15 minutes earlier every day so you have time to connect before the day starts, or more exotic, such as experimenting with something new in the bedroom. You are only limited by your own imaginations.

Each partner should write down new beginnings ideas on sticky notes, put them in plastic Easter egg–type containers, and hide them around the house. Then both partners should search around the house, finding all the eggs (and giving each other clues if they are difficult to find). After all the eggs are found, discuss how the ideas could be implemented.

Supplies Needed: Sticky notes, pens or pencils, and plastic eggs or other small containers

Record the ideas here after you find them:

1. _____

   _____

2. _____

   _____

3. _____

   _____

4. _____

   _____

5. _____

   _____

6. _____

_____

7. _____

_____

8. _____

_____

9. _____

_____

10. _____

_____

Reflect and Plan: After you have discovered all the "new beginnings" eggs, reflect on the ones you like the most. Think about how you can adapt a few of them into bucket list items.

Bucket List Items: _____

_____

_____

KIND WORDS

Share the love and kindness you have for each other with the world! For this activity, sit down together to write inspiring, uplifting, and funny messages on sticky notes or to print out on large sheets of paper. Then brainstorm where you would like to leave these messages in your community, such as at a public bench or the announcement board at your local library or community center. Maybe you can expand upon this idea and create donation bags in which you can leave these messages.

On the same day or another, go out with your partner to leave the messages in the places you brainstormed earlier.

Supplies Needed: Paper or sticky notes, pens or pencils

LOCATIONS

1. _____   6. _____
2. _____   7. _____
3. _____   8. _____
4. _____   9. _____
5. _____   10. _____

MESSAGES

1. _____

_____

2. _____

_____

3. _____

_____

4. _____

_____

5. _____

6. _____

7. _____

8. _____

9. _____

10. _____

11. _____

Reflect and Plan: How did it feel to do this activity? Is it something you would like to expand upon or do more often? In what other ways can you give back to your community together?

Bucket List Item: _____

_____

_____

PET PEEVES

Everyone has small things that bother them in life. Some people are quite happy to let everyone know about them, but others are more likely to keep them to themselves. This is your chance to let it all out. For one minute, each partner can talk (or write) about their biggest pet peeve and why they find it so annoying. Then both partners can work together to try to find a way to lessen or eliminate those pet peeves from each other's lives.

Partner A: _____

_____

_____

Partner B: _____

_____

_____

Reflect and Plan: You might think, "What do pet peeves have to do with a bucket list?" But talking about them is an opportunity: You can create a bucket list out of trying to overcome your annoyance over your pet peeve or around trying to make sure this pet peeve has a reduced role in your life.

Bucket List Items: _____

_____

_____

TOP CHOICES

We all have our preferences. But even if you think you know everything about your partner's likes and dislikes, there's always more to discover!

On separate sheets of paper, each partner should write down at least 10 questions with four possible answers. Then, pass the question and answers to the other partner, asking them to rank the choices. For example, "Rank the ways you would prefer to travel, from most to least favorite: (1) car, (2) air, (3) sea, or (4) train." Or "Rank whether you would prefer to watch: (1) only your favorite show for the rest of your life, (2) only horror movies, (3) only romantic comedies, or (4) no movies, ever."

Supplies Needed: Paper, pens or pencils

Keep a record of your experience here, if you'd like. Did you have some of the same favorites as each other or were they mostly different?

_____

_____

_____

_____

_____

_____

Reflect and Plan: When you've selected your favorites, cut them out and mix them up in a hat or bowl (so each slip of paper might say "a train" or "on a deserted island"). Pick out three at random, and find ways to incorporate whatever they say into your bucket list item.

Bucket List Item: _____

_____

A MEMORY GAME

You probably remember playing the memory game in school. This is like that—except instead of getting a sticker or toy for winning, you get a prize you'd like now!

Cut a few pieces of thick paper (the kind you can't read words through) into 20 pieces and write 10 words on them—each word should be written on two pieces of paper. Don't use markers since you might be able to see the words through the paper. Then put the pieces of paper facedown and take turns flipping two of them over at a time. If you don't match the cards, flip them back over, and your partner gets a turn. When you match two cards, you get a reward!

Here are some ideas for rewards:

* Massage

* Your partner cooks your favorite meal

* Date night of your choice

* Breakfast in bed

* A day to do nothing but relax

Write your own rewards together—whatever is the most fun and exciting to you (in addition to or in place of these suggestions).

Supplies Needed: Thick paper or cardboard, pens or pencils, scissors

REWARD IDEAS

1. _____

2. _____

3. _____

4. _____

5. _____

6. _____

7. _____

8. _____

9. _____

10. _____

Reflect and Plan: Talk about why you chose the rewards that you did. What is special about them? Which do you want to do more of in the future?

Bucket List Item: _____

_____

_____

WHAT WOULD YOU BE?

You know your partner pretty well. But do you know what pet they'd most like to be? Or what superhero?

For this activity, you will guess what your partner would be if they could be anything in certain categories. For example, what body part would your partner be? What movie character, song, tree, pet, type of fabric, food, vehicle, superhero, sport, or cartoon? Pick categories that resonate with you, write down your guesses on separate sheets of paper and then swap the sheets with your partner to see what you each got right! Record your correct guesses here.

CATEGORY	PARTNER A	PARTNER B
Body Part		
Pet		

Reflect and Plan: What do you find exciting and interesting about the choices you made in life? It could be where you live, your career, the friends you chose, or anything else. How can you incorporate more of these exciting choices into your lives?

Bucket List Item: _____

_____

_____

MAGIC

Many of us grow up thinking magic exists only in fairy tales. But what if magic were real? Or do you already think magic exists? Do you think people would use it for good or evil? Would you use it? Discuss your thoughts on magic. Do you have different ideas or similar ones?

Partner A: _____

_____

_____

Partner B: _____

_____

_____

Reflect and Plan: Are there any activities you'd like to try that reflect the concept of magic? Would you try to learn magic or go to a magic show?

Bucket List Items: _____

_____

_____

WORD COMPETITION

It can be fun to have a little healthy competition with your partner, especially when it's playful and low stakes.

Come up with a category. Then, one partner writes down a noun relevant to that category. The other partner tries to think of another noun that could "beat" the first word. For example, if you have a theme of "wild animals," and the first partner writes down "lion," the other needs to come up with an animal that could "beat" a lion—such as a hippo (it's true!). If the theme is "movie characters," Thor might beat Superman. Think of your own categories and engage in a ridiculous debate about who wins!

CATEGORY	PARTNER A	PARTNER B
Wild animals		
Movie characters		

Reflect and Plan: What do you find most intriguing about these categories? Are they tied to your passions? Do they represent areas of your lives or the world you'd like to explore more?

Bucket List Item: _____

_____

_____

DO-OVERS

We have all made mistakes in our lives. Some are insignificant while others may have altered the course of your life, for better or for worse. Either way, we can all learn something from looking at our past mistakes.

But sometimes, the fact that we grew from our mistake doesn't matter to us; instead, we wish we could take a time machine back and get a do-over.

That's what this prompt is all about. Is there a moment in your life that you would like a do-over for? What happened? Why did you do what you did at the time? Was it intentional or an accident? What did you learn from this incident? Did it make you a better person? What would you do differently?

Partner A: _____

_____

_____

_____

_____

_____

Partner B: _____

_____

_____

_____

_____

_____

_____

Reflect and Plan: What's a small do-over activity that you can plan together?

Bucket List Item: _____

_____

LOTTERY WIN

Imagine that the "impossible" happened—you won the lottery! Think about the thrill of that, how exciting it would be!

Talk or write with your partner about what each of you would do if you won $1 million or more in the lottery. Would you spend it on material things, such as a bigger house or nicer car? Or would you use it for experiences, such as travel? How much of it would you give away to other people or charities? Focus on the meaning of money—what does it represent to you? Freedom? Prestige? Security? Or something else?

Partner A: _____

_____

_____

Partner B: _____

_____

_____

Reflect and Plan: Just because you don't win the lottery doesn't mean that you can't accomplish some of the things you'd do if you won. Which ones are the most important to you? How can you take small steps toward achieving them?

Bucket List Items: _____

_____

_____

THE "I'VE NEVER" GUESSING GAME

We all have things that we haven't done. Sometimes, that's because we just haven't had the opportunity to do so; other times, it's because we simply don't want to do it. You can learn a lot about your partner by learning not just what they have done but also what they haven't.

On separate sheets of paper, each partner should write down at least 10 things that they have never done before. They can be simple things, such as "I've never eaten shrimp" or more elaborate, such as "I've never tried belly dancing." Keep your list to yourself but give your partner a hint about your first item. Continue to provide hints as they guess. Then switch off and try to guess one of their items. Go back and forth.

Supplies Needed: Paper, pens or pencils

Keep a record of your experience here, if you'd like. How did it feel to reveal to each other some of the things you have never done?

_____

_____

_____

_____

_____

_____

_____

Reflect and Plan: Go through each "I never" item and talk about why you have never done it. Is it by choice or not? Which ones do you want to try?

Bucket List Item: _____

_____

_____

A STORY OF OUR OWN

Many of us haven't used our creative writing skills since we were in school. But flexing your creativity with your partner can help you feel closer and gain new insights into each other.

Decide on the type of story you two would most like to write. Are you interested in romance, a horror story, or maybe science fiction?

Next, talk about your favorite novels and what you liked about them. This will help you think about what makes a story appealing to each of you.

Finally, it's time to work on your own story. You can write a super-short story—even just a paragraph can work—or simply develop the characteristics of your main characters.

OUR STORY

_____

_____

_____

_____

_____

_____

_____

_____

_____

_____

_____

_____

_____

_____

_____

_____

_____

_____

_____

_____

_____

_____

_____

_____

_____

_____

_____

_____

_____

_____

_____

_____

_____

_____

_____

_____

_____

_____

_____

_____

_____

_____

_____

Reflect and Plan: What other fun, unusual things can you do as a team?

Bucket List Item: _____

_____

_____

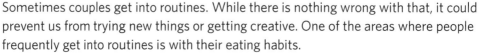

NEW RECIPE

Sometimes couples get into routines. While there is nothing wrong with that, it could prevent us from trying new things or getting creative. One of the areas where people frequently get into routines is with their eating habits.

This activity is all about creating or inventing a new recipe together. Don't even consult a cookbook or the internet because this is meant for you to collaborate on making some new and tasty dish. Then come up with a theme and name for a fictional restaurant where you'd serve the food. Finally, cook the recipe and serve it at a romantic dinner for two!

Supplies Needed: Food, spices, cooking utensils—basically, your kitchen!

Name of dish: _____

Theme: _____

Name of restaurant: _____

Ingredients:

1. _____
2. _____
3. _____
4. _____
5. _____
6. _____
7. _____
8. _____
9. _____
10. _____

Steps:

1. _____
2. _____
3. _____
4. _____
5. _____
6. _____
7. _____
8. _____
9. _____
10. _____

Reflect and Plan: What kinds of cuisines do you most enjoy? How can you try to experience new foods in an exciting way?

Bucket List Items: _____

_____

_____

VISION BOARD

Create a vision board for your future together. You can envision far into the future or just a few months out. Make a list of categories that are important to you for the long-term future, such as family, finances, careers, and retirement, or for the short term, such as a list of places to go, activities to try, and dates to plan. Search for and print out images representing these categories or cut them out of magazines. Paste, tape, or pin them on a big poster or corkboard. Feel free to decorate your vision board with messages to each other or pictures of you together.

As you go through this activity, take the time to have slow, thoughtful conversations about your goals, dreams, and wants. Be gentle, generous, and open with each other.

Supplies Needed: Posterboard, corkboard, or cardboard; glue, tape, or thumbtacks; magazines and/or internet

Write down some key takeaways from your conversation together so that you can continue to discuss later on, if you'd like.

_____

_____

_____

_____

_____

_____

_____

Reflect and Plan: What are some of the things on the vision board that you are really excited about it? Will you make them into bucket list items and commit to getting them done?

Bucket List Item: _____

_____

_____

GREAT MINDS THINK ALIKE! OR DO THEY?

Do you basically share a brain with your partner or are you pretty different? For the following questions, on separate sheets of paper, see if you write down the same answer. Continue to add questions if you want.

1. Best cheese for grilled sandwich?

2. Ketchup on top of the french fries or on the side?

3. Hang toilet paper over or under?

4. Ice cream or frozen yogurt?

5. Cake or pie?

6. Cups in the cupboard: right-side up or upside down?

7. Blinds or curtain?

8. Classical art or modern art?

9. Card game or board game?

10. Sweater or hoodie?

Supplies Needed: Paper, pens or pencils

Reflect and Plan: Many couples focus on their differences and not enough on their similarities. Think about the list you just created and how you can create a unique activity based on the ones you agree on.

Bucket List Item: _____

_____

_____

SONG MEMORIES

Music defines a lot of our lives. Not only do many of our favorite songs have meaningful lyrics, but they also bring back memories from our lives when we hear them.

Find five songs from your childhood (or more recent past) that bring back specific memories. Play these songs for your partner, and then talk about what memories you have from that time in your life. It could be a school dance or a first date. Try to choose songs that have both happy and not-so-happy memories attached to them. Sharing the emotions you felt during these times will bring the two of you closer.

Supplies Needed: Smartphone or computer, internet, paper, pens or pencils

PARTNER A'S SONGS

1. _____

2. _____

3. _____

4. _____

5. _____

Thoughts: _____

_____

_____

_____

_____

_____

PARTNER B'S SONGS

1. _____
2. _____
3. _____
4. _____
5. _____

Thoughts: _____

_____

_____

_____

_____

_____

_____

Reflect and Plan: What kinds of memories would you like to relive? What kinds of memories do you want to make in the future that would involve listening to songs?

Bucket List Items: _____

_____

_____

MYSTERY CHARACTER GAME

This is a guessing game and writing activity all rolled up into one! Each of you should choose a well-known fictional character or a celebrity. Do not tell your partner who you chose.

Next, write down the qualities of this character or celebrity. They can be anything, such as their race or gender, their profession, their family, their famous quotes, or anything else that would describe them. Be careful not to make it too obvious so your partner will be challenged a bit to guess correctly. Then each partner can try to guess whom the other partner picked.

Repeat this as many times as you like, and keep score to see who can guess the most characters.

PARTNER A'S CHARACTER(S)

1. _____

_____

_____

_____

2. _____

_____

_____

_____

3. _____

_____

_____

_____

PARTNER B'S CHARACTER(S)

1. _____
   _____
   _____
   _____

2. _____
   _____
   _____
   _____

3. _____
   _____
   _____
   _____

SCORES

Partner A: _____

Partner B: _____

Reflect and Plan: There's a lot that you don't necessarily know—about the world, or even about what your partner is thinking. What are some fun ways you can engage with all the things that you don't know?

Bucket List Item: _____
_____
_____

ROLL OF THE DICE

This activity is for making a list of things that you can do at a later date . . . but leaving it all to chance, with the roll of the dice!

Write out two lists. On one list, write six actions and number them, such as:

1. Dance

2. Drink

3. Play

4. Eat

5. Laugh

6. Learn

On the other list, write six places, such as:

1. The mall

2. Miniature golf course

3. Backyard

4. Bowling alley

5. Fast-food restaurant

6. School

Once you've completed the lists, roll your two dice together, and combine the corresponding items from each list. For example, if you roll a 1 and a 5, then you will "Dance at a fast-food restaurant." Keep rolling until you have a long list of fun, silly ideas.

Supplies Needed: Two 6-sided dice (preferably different colors)

ACTIONS

1. _____
2. _____
3. _____
4. _____
5. _____
6. _____

PLACES

1. _____
2. _____
3. _____
4. _____
5. _____
6. _____

Reflect and Plan: Can you take this approach to some bucket list activities, too, and add them to the list?

Bucket List Item: _____

_____

_____

TRUTHS AND LIES

Even if you've known your partner for decades, there are still some things you probably don't know about each other. For example, maybe in the third grade, you slipped and fell in front of your whole class. You may not have told your partner, though not necessarily on purpose—it probably just never came up.

For this activity, each partner should write down two true statements about themselves and one lie. The other partner then must guess which one is the lie. Take turns doing this, and go as many rounds as you want to!

Supplies Needed: Paper, pens or pencils

PARTNER A

1. _____

   _____

2. _____

   _____

3. _____

   _____

PARTNER B

1. _____

   _____

2. _____

   _____

3. _____

   _____

Reflect and Plan: Look at some of the lies you told. They may be based in your desires (such as "I sang in a rock band"). How can you explore these desires in real life?

Bucket List Item: _____

_____

_____

TABOO WORDS

Have you ever noticed that as soon as someone tells you, "Don't think of a purple elephant," that's all you can think about? This game does the same with words.

    Each partner should choose three COMMON words that the other one can't say, such as "car" or "sky." These are the "taboo" words. Then begin having a conversation, with each partner making sure that they don't say any of the words that their partner has listed as taboo.

    If you say one of the words, your partner gets a point. If they say one of your taboo words, then you get a point. Each person should try to avoid their partner's taboo words while trying to get their partner to say their taboo words. Set a timer for 10 minutes, and when it goes off, whoever has the most points wins!

NUMBER OF TIMES PARTNER A SAID TABOO WORDS

1. Taboo word no. 1: _____

2. Taboo word no. 2: _____

3. Taboo word no. 3: _____

NUMBER OF TIMES PARTNER B SAID TABOO WORDS

1. Taboo word no. 1: _____

2. Taboo word no. 2: _____

3. Taboo word no. 3: _____

Reflect and Plan: What else in your life is generally forbidden or taboo? Is there a way to have safe fun enjoying one of these forbidden or taboo things?

Bucket List Item: _____

_____

_____

GUESS THE NUMBER

Each partner should look around the house and find something that can be counted. Then you will create a contest to see who is able to get closest to the real number.

You should choose different categories, such as:

* Number of pens in your junk drawer
* Number of photos you have on your phone
* Number of months you have been alive
* Number of texts you exchanged last week
* Number of days you have known each other
* Number of extended family members between the two of you
* Number of shoes in your closet
* Number of bowls in your cabinet
* Number of unread books or magazines

Whoever comes closest to the real number gets one point. Whoever has the most points at the end is the winner.

Supplies Needed: Paper, pens or pencil

THINGS THAT CAN BE COUNTED

1. _____
2. _____
3. _____
4. _____
5. _____
6. _____
7. _____
8. _____
9. _____
10. _____

PARTNER A

1. _____
2. _____
3. _____
4. _____
5. _____
6. _____
7. _____
8. _____
9. _____
10. _____

PARTNER B

1. _____
2. _____
3. _____
4. _____
5. _____
6. _____
7. _____
8. _____
9. _____
10. _____

SCORES

Partner A: _____

Partner B: _____

Reflect and Plan: Talk about why you have the things you have. Why do you have so many or so few? What does that say about you two, your priorities, and your interests?

Bucket List Item: _____

_____

_____

KEEPING SCORE

While it can be fun to watch or play sports such as basketball or football, it's even more fun to come up with a new and different one, designed by the two of you.

Start out by discussing what you like the most about sports in general. Do you like the competition? The physical experience? The intellectual challenge? And what don't you like? Use these preferences to guide your imagination, then write down a few rules of your game. Does it involve a ball? Take place on a field? What's the objective?

Once you have designed the sport, give it a name. Brainstorm some names, and then choose your favorite. If you want, you can even try to play a round of the game!

Overall concept of the sport: _____

_____

_____

_____

_____

Number of players: _____

_____

Equipment used: _____

_____

Scoring system: _____

_____

Name of sport: _____

Reflect and Plan: What else can you create from scratch together?

Bucket List Item: _____

_____

PET NAMES

Many of us go by nicknames instead of full names—like "Bec" for "Rebecca" or "Maggie" for "Margaret." Couples tend to come up with their own special names for each other, too, though they don't always have to do with full names—more often, they're closer to "honey," "babe," or "sweetie."

Having pet names for each other can increase emotional intimacy. The goal of this activity is to brainstorm and find a cute, funny, or new pet name you can start calling your partner. Come up with as many funny/strange pet names you can think of for each partner.

NAMES FOR PARTNER A	NAMES FOR PARTNER B
1.	1.
2.	2.
3.	3.
4.	4.
5.	5.
6.	6.
7.	7.
8.	8.
9.	9.
10.	10.

Reflect and Plan: What do you like or not like about these names? What parts of your life or personality to do they represent? How did they make you feel: happy, closer, silly? Were they inspired by something meaningful that you would like to explore more of?

Bucket List Item: _____

_____

_____

TREASURE CHEST

What do you treasure most in the world? It doesn't have to be an object. It could be people, animals, qualities, or special moments. After making a list of your treasures, choose something from your list that has an interesting story behind it. Did you win it? Was it given to you by someone special? Did you earn it through hard work? Share the story with your partner!

PARTNER A	PARTNER B
1. _____	1. _____
2. _____	2. _____
3. _____	3. _____
4. _____	4. _____
5. _____	5. _____
6. _____	6. _____
7. _____	7. _____
8. _____	8. _____
9. _____	9. _____
10. _____	10. _____

Reflect and Plan: Look over your lists. Is there something you can start collecting? Or maybe you want to start a new collection that has meaning for the both of you. Where can this search or effort take you?

Bucket List Items: _____

_____

_____

CONVERSATION CONTEST

Even if you always find it fun to talk to your partner, this game might inject some more lightness and humor into it.

One of you starts a conversation by making a statement or asking a question. The other one must answer by using the last letter of the last word in the sentence. Then the first partner must continue the conversation using that letter.

Here's an example:

Partner A: "What is your favorite restaurant?" (letter T)

Partner B: "The restaurant I like the most is Tom's Burger Shack." (letter K)

Partner A: "Knowing that, maybe we should plan a trip there in the next day or two." (letter O)

Whoever can't think of a way to continue the conversation loses. Try a few rounds, and keep track of your scores.

SCORES

Partner A: _____

Partner B: _____

Reflect and Plan: What do you like the most about having conversations? How can you make sure you have more in your relationship?

Bucket List Items: _____

_____

_____

MOVING LYRICS

Music is a huge part of many people's lives, but how often do you listen closely to or read the words and think about the emotions behind the songs?

Choose some of your favorite songs and play them for each other. Pay close attention to the lyrics. Do you hear anything unexpected now that you're paying close attention to them?

What events in the person's life do you think might have led to their creating the song?

Then write about the emotions the lyrics specifically stir up. Are they different from the feelings the overall song creates in you?

PARTNER A'S FAVORITE SONGS

1. _____

2. _____

3. _____

4. _____

5. _____

Thoughts: _____

_____

_____

_____

_____

_____

PARTNER B'S FAVORITE SONGS

1. _____
2. _____
3. _____
4. _____
5. _____

Thoughts: _____

_____

_____

_____

_____

_____

_____

Reflect and Plan: Did any of the lyrics inspire you? Did they make you remember something you want to experience? Or would you perhaps want to try to write song lyrics together?

Bucket List Item: _____

_____

_____

WHY, YOU ARE AWESOME!

You have likely told your partner many things you love about them. But there may be some other, not-so-obvious qualities that you admire in them but have never specifically mentioned.

In this activity, each partner should tell the other about a quality of theirs that they admire but have never mentioned before. You can also write it down. They can be big ("You have a very generous heart") or small ("You always pick the best movies to watch"). Focus on things that are unique about them and that they probably didn't even know you had given much thought to.

Partner A: _____

_____

_____

Partner B: _____

_____

_____

Reflect and Plan: Talk about these qualities and how you both could have an experience that really makes those qualities shine.

Bucket List Items: _____

_____

_____

SCIENCE FICTION AND FACT

Pretend that you are scientists who have discovered how to teleport yourselves anywhere instantly. You could go halfway across the world, or even to a different planet, in the blink of an eye. What places would be the most intriguing and exciting for you to visit? Would you stay on Earth or travel to a distant planet? Each partner should write down their thoughts and then share.

If you had the opportunity to invent technologies that could significantly change your life and the lives of everyone in the world, what would you want to invent? Discuss what you'd both like to create and if you think it will ever be invented.

Partner A: _____

_____

_____

Partner B: _____

_____

_____

Reflect and Plan: What problems did you want to solve with your inventions? Could you work on solving those problems right now, even just a little?

Bucket List Item: _____

_____

_____

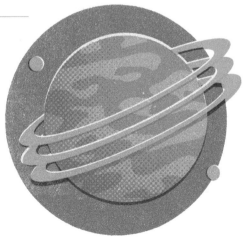

TOP LIKES AND DISLIKES

Our passions and our pet peeves are unique; no two of us have the same ones. Sometimes, we keep these to ourselves because letting others know what we love (or hate!) makes us feel too vulnerable. But to understand your partner on a deeper level, it's important to know what they love and hate. That's why, in this activity, you'll each rank your top-five likes and dislikes.

You don't have to limit yourself to any certain category. For example, you could list your favorite films, favorite and least favorite foods, personal habits that annoy you—the sky's the limit!

PARTNER A
Likes:

1. _____

2. _____

3. _____

4. _____

5. _____

Dislikes:

1. _____

2. _____

3. _____

4. _____

5. _____

PARTNER B
Likes:

1. _____
2. _____
3. _____
4. _____
5. _____

Dislikes:

1. _____
2. _____
3. _____
4. _____
5. _____

Reflect and Plan: After you share your likes and dislikes with your partner, brainstorm ways you can share your likes more with each other—or challenge your dislikes in a fun way.

Bucket List Item: _____

_____

_____

YOU, AS A CHILD

Many people did not know their partners when they were children. You may think you know what kind of kid they were … but do you really?

For this activity, each partner should gather some old photos of themselves to show each other. This can be done at home or through photo apps or social media platforms in which you have uploaded photos for a long time. Next, each partner should write down some questions about themselves to help the other guess what they were like as children (from birth to 18). Here are some examples:

✳ How did I stop believing in Santa?

✳ What kind of grades did I get?

✳ Did I have a lot of close friends or a few close friends?

✳ What was my favorite outfit or clothing style?

✳ What was my least favorite haircut?

Supplies Needed: Paper, pens or pencils

PARTNER A'S QUESTIONS

1. _____

2. _____

3. _____

4. _____

5. _____

PARTNER B'S QUESTIONS

1. _____
   _____

2. _____
   _____

3. _____
   _____

4. _____
   _____

5. _____
   _____

Reflect and Plan: What would you change about yourself as a child, if anything? Would you have been more daring or risk-taking? Or is there something you cherish from childhood that you would like to experience again?

Bucket List Item: _____

_____

_____

PAST AND FUTURE SUCCESSES

Think back on your life. What would you consider your greatest successes? What are you most proud of? Why?

Each partner should write a list of successes—as many as each can think of. Then swap lists.

Talk about why you are so proud of these accomplishments. How did they make you feel? Did they take a lot of effort to accomplish? Did they come as a surprise, or did you work hard for them?

Next, think about the rest of your life and what you want to accomplish. What goals and dreams do you have right now that you hope become future successes? Each partner should make a list of these, too. Make sure you keep them in a prominent spot, to remind you to take action in the future.

PARTNER A

Past Successes: _____

_____

_____

_____

_____

_____

Future Successes: _____

_____

_____

_____

_____

_____

PARTNER B

Past Successes: _____

_____

_____

_____

_____

_____

_____

Future Successes: _____

_____

_____

_____

_____

_____

_____

Reflect and Plan: What activities can help move you closer to these future goals?

Bucket List Item: _____

_____

_____

WEEKLY PLAN

Many of us plan the week ahead so we can stay on top of work duties or obligations related to children's activities or family get-togethers. But how often do you plan fun?

In this activity, schedule one unique or unusual thing that you and your partner can do together every day for one week. Think outside the box and come up with something wild or silly to make your week a little more exciting than usual.

Day 1: _____

_____

_____

Day 2: _____

_____

_____

Day 3: _____

_____

_____

Day 4: _____

_____

_____

Day 5: _____

_____

_____

Day 6: _____

_____

_____

Day 7: _____

_____

_____

Reflect and Plan: Talk about how you can make every week a little different from the others. Are there any activities you want to incorporate into your life on a more regular basis?

Bucket List Item: _____

_____

_____

FIVE RANDOM THINGS

This prompt is all about quick reactions and honest opinions. First, each think of at least two or three categories. Here are some ideas to get you started:

* What I want us to do this month

* What I appreciate about you

* What I want to do for you

* Places I want us to visit this year

For each category, write the first five things that come to mind. Get creative—not only with the answers but also with the categories. And while you do, think about how you can tie these into a bucket list item.

CATEGORY	PARTNER A	PARTNER B

CATEGORY	PARTNER A	PARTNER B

CATEGORY	PARTNER A	PARTNER B

CATEGORY	PARTNER A	PARTNER B

Reflect and Plan: Which items on the list sound the most interesting or exciting?

Bucket List Items: _____

_____

_____

AWARD SPEECH

The flashing lights, the shiny jewelry, the people screaming your name. Being famous sounds very glamorous, and a lot of people in the world would like to experience it. However, there are advantages and disadvantages to everything in life—even fame.

Talk to each other about what it would be like to be so famous that you won an important award. When receiving this award, you are required to give a meaningful speech. What would you like to win the award for, and what kinds of things would you say while accepting it?

Write the highlights of the speech here, and then trade highlights with each other.

Partner A: _____

_____

_____

Partner B: _____

_____

_____

Reflect and Plan: Are there any steps you can take to get closer to your dream of accomplishing something that you really care about?

Bucket List Item: _____

_____

_____

RISKY OFFER

Some people love taking risks; others are afraid of them. Many risks offer rewards, though some do not and may just give you a temporary thrill.

    Imagine something that you are extremely afraid of doing. It could be something physically risky, like skydiving or bungee jumping, or something emotionally risky, like speaking in front of thousands of people. Each partner should write down one of their most-feared risks. Would you do what you fear for a certain amount of money? If so, how much money would it take for you to do it? Are there risks you would not take for any amount of money?

Partner A: _____

_____

_____

Partner B: _____

_____

_____

Reflect and Plan: Talk about what risk-taking means to you. What are your boundaries for taking a risk? What risks have you taken in the past that you are happy that you did? Do you want to incorporate more healthy risk-taking into your life?

Bucket List Items: _____

_____

_____

PERFECT HAPPINESS

The concept of happiness is so personal that even longtime couples may not have the same definition.

Each partner should write down a number of things that make them happy in life. Don't discuss them ahead of time; just write them down and share them when you are both done. Then talk about them, making sure to ask questions about why particular things bring your partner such happiness. You can also get deep by asking questions such as, "If you could live one year in perfect happiness but not remember it when the year was over, would you do it?"

PARTNER A

1. _____
2. _____
3. _____
4. _____
5. _____
6. _____
7. _____
8. _____
9. _____
10. _____

PARTNER B

1. _____
2. _____
3. _____
4. _____
5. _____
6. _____
7. _____
8. _____
9. _____
10. _____

Reflect and Plan: Think about whether you are doing enough to make yourself and your partner as happy as possible. How can you introduce more of the things that make you happy into your regular life?

Bucket List Items: _____

_____

_____

UNCOMMON QUESTIONS

In daily life, conversation usually hinges on topics related to work, family, and news. But how often do you get into weird, deep, and unexpected conversations with your partner? If you've never done that before, now is your chance!

Write down as many offbeat questions as you can think of. Examples could be "What ridiculous thing has someone tricked you into doing or believing?" or "What's the closest thing to real magic?" Anything goes! Get as wild as you can. Then ask each other your questions and see what kind of conversation ensues.

PARTNER A

1. _____

_____

2. _____

_____

3. _____

_____

4. _____

_____

5. _____

_____

6. _____

_____

7. _____

_____

8. _____

_____

9. _____

_____

10. _____

_____

PARTNER B

1. _____

2. _____

3. _____

4. _____

5. _____

6. _____

7. _____

8. _____

9. _____

10. _____

Reflect and Plan: As you go through the questions, ask follow-up ones. Probe deeper into your partner's mind and heart to try to understand their answers. Does this unusual thinking lead you to any new, unexpected bucket list items?

Bucket List Item: _____

_____

FAVORITE AGE

Growing up and aging can be both fun and difficult—sometimes at the same time. Hopefully, every era of our lives is full of positive memories, but many of us have a favorite age or period of our lives.

This activity provides you with the opportunity to really look back on your life and reflect on your favorite era or age (within a two- or three-year period). Focus on the times when you felt the best about yourself and/or when you learned the most about life. Write down the highlights and the things that changed you.

Partner A: _____

_____

_____

_____

_____

Partner B: _____

_____

_____

_____

_____

Reflect and Plan: Talk about why you enjoyed this age or phase of life so much. What did you accomplish? What were you proud of? How can you do more of that kind of thing in the future?

Bucket List Items: _____

_____

_____

ICEBREAKERS

Regardless of how long you have known each other, there will always be something about your partner that you do not know. Whether it's about childhood, their work life, or something else, there's always something new to learn.

For this prompt, pretend that you and your partner are on a blind date. This is your chance to have a second icebreaker moment in your relationship. You could ask your partner specific questions about things you want to know, or you can let them decide what unknown things they want to share with you. Either way, you're sure to learn something new.

Keep a record of your experience here, if you'd like. How did it feel to be on this "blind" date?

_____

_____

_____

_____

_____

_____

_____

Reflect and Plan: Did you learn anything surprising about your partner? Information about things they love or are fearful of but want to overcome? Think about these new things you learned and how you can make them into a shared and unique experience.

Bucket List Items: _____

_____

_____

DECISIONS, DECISIONS

We make tons of decisions throughout our lives, but most of them are relatively small. This activity asks you to look inside and make some BIG decisions. (Even though it's all theoretical, it will still help you learn more about each other.)

Each partner should write down two different things and ask the other which one they would choose to keep in the world and which one they would eliminate entirely. Some examples are:

* Traffic jams OR waiting in long lines

* Failure OR stress

* Summer OR winter

* Forests OR oceans

Start by brainstorming categories to create the "either-or" options.

PARTNER A

1. _____

   OR _____

2. _____

   OR _____

3. _____

   OR _____

4. _____

   OR _____

5. _____

   OR _____

PARTNER B

1. _____
   OR _____
2. _____
   OR _____
3. _____
   OR _____
4. _____
   OR _____
5. _____
   OR _____

Reflect and Plan: Talk about whether there is anything you can actually do to make a difference in any of these categories. Are there some small steps you could take?

Bucket List Item: _____

_____

_____

TALENT SHOW

Make a list of your talents! If you're having a hard time coming up with a few, ask your partner. Then select one from your list to practice and show off in a talent show. Yes, a talent show! Grow this activity into bigger fun by planning a talent show with your friends and family. Even if you are feeling a little shy, challenge yourself to step out of your comfort zone, or plan a talent show with those you are truly comfortable with.

PARTNER A'S TALENTS

1. _____
2. _____
3. _____

PARTNER B'S TALENTS

1. _____
2. _____
3. _____

Reflect and Plan: Talk about these talents you have and if you have incorporated any of them into your everyday life. If not, how can you do it more? Or how can you create a once-in-a-lifetime experience with your talents?

Bucket List Items: _____

_____

_____

A VERY UNUSUAL TRIP TO THE BEACH

Imagine that you are on a vacation and heading toward a beach. The sand and the surf are mesmerizing, and it's fun to do a little people watching, too.

But what if you and your partner walked onto this beach and discovered, much to your surprise, that it was a nudist beach? That's right—not one stitch of clothing or swimsuit in sight. What would you do? Would you eagerly strip and join the nudists? Or would you be self-conscious and keep your suit on?

Partner A: _____

_____

_____

Partner B: _____

_____

_____

Reflect and Plan: Would you put going to a nudist beach on your bucket list? This experience would be very out of some people's comfort zones. What else could you do that is out of your comfort zones?

Bucket List Items: _____

_____

_____

COMING CLEAN

At some point in our lives, many of us will tell a white lie—a small untruth that doesn't feel as dishonest as a major lie. Although it's not easy to disclose that you've been untruthful in the past, admitting it can cleanse the soul, so to speak. This prompt will help you do that—and bring you and your partner closer in the process.

Write down some of the lies you each have told in your lives, both big and small. Try not to judge yourself or each other for them. Instead, have empathy and compassion, and talk about why you lied when you did.

PARTNER A

1. _____

_____

2. _____

_____

3. _____

_____

4. _____

_____

5. _____

_____

PARTNER B

1. _____

_____

2. _____

_____

3. _____

_____

4. _____

_____

5. _____

_____

Reflect and Plan: Reflect on the idea of forgiveness. How would it feel to give it? To receive it? Is forgiving part of any bucket list activity?

Bucket List Item: _____

_____

_____

MAKE YOUR OWN MIRACLE

Many people hope for miracles in their lives—sudden, enormous changes that make a huge difference. If you could have a miracle occur in your life, what would it be? Why would you choose it?

This prompt helps you probe into your dreams and desires—not just for yourselves but also for the world. It will also help you understand what your partner needs to be happy, not only in the relationship but in life.

Partner A: _____

_____

_____

Partner B: _____

_____

_____

Reflect and Plan: Generally, people think of a miracle as something that can never happen or is highly unlikely. But maybe some of the miracles you dream of are possible, in whole or in part. Are there any steps you can take to bring them closer to being realized?

Bucket List Items: _____

_____

_____

A PORTRAIT OF YOU

This activity is for couples who may be looking to try something daring or to push each other outside their comfort zones. Pose for each other completely naked and sketch, draw, or paint each other on paper or canvas.

You can be more artistic with these portraits by placing meaningful items around you or draping a sheet over parts of your body. Take the time to adjust lights, set the mood, and do whatever else makes each other comfortable and empowered in your bodies. Don't forget to compliment each other as well!

Supplies Needed: Your choice of art supplies: paper, pencils, canvas, paintbrushes, paint, markers, charcoal; candles, sheets, or other accessories

Keep a record of your experience here, if you'd like. Were there any artistic triumphs or challenges as you went through the activity?

_____

_____

_____

_____

_____

_____

Reflect and Plan: How did it feel and what thoughts ran through your mind as you posed or painted? Did you feel vulnerable? Creative? Powerful? How did your partner take care of you? In what ways can you improve or replicate this experience?

Bucket List Item: _____

_____

CHILDHOOD FAVORITES

It's likely that you didn't know your partner as a child. Though you have probably heard stories about their childhood, you may not really know what they were like or what they were passionate about.

Here are some categories you can guess in—try to imagine their favorites and make a list:

* Books
* Movies
* TV shows
* Food
* Drinks
* Hobbies

Have your partner make a list about you as well. Then swap them. How accurate were they in describing you as a child? What did you get right and wrong? Was their list about you accurate?

Supplies Needed: Paper, pens or pencils

Reflect and Plan: Talk about whether your personality and interests have changed over the years. What did you enjoy as a child that you still enjoy now?

Bucket List Item: _____

_____

_____

CAN YOU READ MY FACE?

Time to make faces at each other! From this list of emotions or moods, one partner chooses one to express through their face at their partner. The other partner must guess the emotion. Give yourself a point if you guess correctly, and see who wins at the end. As you go through the list, make sure to cross off the emotions or moods you've already expressed.

EMOTIONS OR MOODS

1. Exasperated
2. Radiant
3. Infatuated
4. Loving
5. Surprised
6. Mischievous
7. Disgusted
8. Excited
9. Charmed
10. Frustrated
11. Calm
12. Nervous
13. Jealous
14. Hopeful
15. Whimsical

SCORES

Partner A: _____

Partner B: _____

Reflect and Plan: Which emotion or mood would you like to experience more of? What are some things you can do to make that happen?

Bucket List Item: _____

_____

_____

A REASON TO CELEBRATE

Holidays are an important part of many of our lives. But some of us simply celebrate the ones that everyone else does—Christmas, Hanukkah, Valentine's Day, Halloween, Diwali, and so on. But you have your own special moments you want to remember—which is why it's time for you and your partner to create your own holidays!

First, think about what kind of holiday you'd like to invent. Do you want it to be romantic? Spooky? Adventurous? Sentimental? Will giving gifts or any other activity be required? It's important to agree on an overall theme, and then you can come up with the specifics.

CELEBRATION 1

Name: _____

Date: _____

What it celebrates: _____
_____

How it is celebrated: _____
_____
_____
_____
_____
_____

CELEBRATION 2

Name: _____

Date: _____

What it celebrates: _____

_____

How it is celebrated: _____

_____

_____

_____

_____

_____

_____

Reflect and Plan: Also consider whether this new holiday is something you would like to celebrate as a couple or if you would like to include other family members and friends, too.

Bucket List Item: _____

_____

_____

WHAT IF?

Do you ever think, *What if?* What if you had gone to a different college when you were younger? How would your life have changed? What if you leave your job and pursue a new career? Would your life be better or worse?

Write down as many what-ifs as you can think of. Then talk to each other about them. What about your life would have turned out differently if these what-ifs had happened? Do you have any regrets? How can you prevent having any regrets in the future?

PARTNER A

1. _____
_____
_____

2. _____
_____
_____

3. _____
_____
_____

4. _____
_____
_____

5. _____
_____
_____

PARTNER B

1. _____
   _____
   _____

2. _____
   _____
   _____

3. _____
   _____
   _____

4. _____
   _____
   _____

5. _____
   _____
   _____

Reflect and Plan: You can't do anything about your past what-ifs, but you can do something to prevent future ones! Think about how you can do some bold things so you can minimize your regrets in the future.

Bucket List Items: _____

_____

_____

GHOST STORIES

When you were a kid, you may have heard ghost stories at sleepover parties or summer camp, or from an older sibling. Now is your chance to revisit those wholesome scares and a childhood tradition.

Start out by talking about your belief in ghosts or the supernatural (or lack thereof). Why do you believe what you believe? Have you ever had a creepy experience? If not, what's one you've heard of and hope never happens to you? Then think about the scariest movies you've seen to get some inspiration. Finally, write one ghost story together, or each create your own and tell them to each other.

PARTNER A

Reasons I could believe ghosts exist:

_____

_____

_____

_____

_____

Reasons I am skeptical about why ghosts do/don't exist:

_____

_____

_____

_____

_____

PARTNER B
Reasons I could believe ghosts exist:

_____

_____

_____

_____

_____

_____

_____

Reasons I am skeptical about why ghosts do/don't exist:

_____

_____

_____

_____

_____

_____

_____

Reflect and Plan: What other beliefs could you explore or challenge together?

Bucket List Item: _____

_____

CONFESSIONS

Regardless of how emotionally intimate a relationship feels, we sometimes keep some things to ourselves. But if you confess some of your most innermost thoughts, it can bring you closer.

Take turns asking each other questions that you want to know the truth about. It could be anything from "Did you ever steal candy as kid?" to "What would you like to do that no one would ever expect of you?" You have the right to refuse the question if you'd like. Take a moment to acknowledge each other's boundaries, and you can move to the next question.

PARTNER A

1. _____

_____

_____

2. _____

_____

_____

3. _____

_____

_____

4. _____

_____

_____

5. _____

_____

_____

PARTNER B

1. _____
   _____
   _____

2. _____
   _____
   _____

3. _____
   _____
   _____

4. _____
   _____
   _____

5. _____
   _____
   _____

Reflect and Plan: How did these answers make you feel closer? Did they reveal any hidden interests that could make a good bucket list item?

Bucket List Items: _____
_____
_____

NO ONE IS WATCHING

Many of us are trustworthy when we know other people are watching what we do. But what if you faced a moral dilemma that no one else would ever know about?

   Talk about different scenarios where you might be tempted to not do the right thing. For example, what if you found $5,000 cash on the sidewalk in the middle of the night when no one was around—would you keep it? What if you accidentally dented a car and no one saw? Each partner should write down at least one scenario for the other to answer.

Partner A: _____

_____

_____

Partner B: _____

_____

_____

Reflect and Plan: Talk about your boundaries and ethics. How can you each become better at living your ethics in the world?

Bucket List Item: _____

_____

_____

INCREASE YOUR IQ?

Imagine that you had the power to increase your IQ to an extremely high genius level. Would you want to do that? What would the advantages or disadvantages be? What if you had to give up something in order to be that smart, such as having access to the internet or having a job?

Alternatively, imagine there is a pill you could take to make you a genius for only 24 hours. What do you think you would do with that intelligence if you had the chance? Would it even be worth it to you if you had it taken away so suddenly?

Write down and talk about the advantages and disadvantages of being a genius.

Partner A: _____

_____

_____

Partner B: _____

_____

_____

Reflect and Plan: Think about the accomplishments of very successful people and/or geniuses in the world. What do you admire about them? How can you emulate some of their successes and have some fun with it along the way?

Bucket List Item: _____

_____

_____

FEAR FACTORS

Everyone has fears, even if they don't like to talk about them. But fears are a part of life and a part of who each of us is as a person. Plus, sharing your fears with each other will increase your vulnerability, enabling you to get to know and understand each other on a deeper level and create a stronger bond.

For this activity, write down at least five of your fears. Make sure to touch on all kinds of fears, such as a fear of spiders or a fear of flying or drowning. Then talk about how these fears developed and whether you think you'll ever move past them. Are there other fears you once had but have moved past?

PARTNER A	PARTNER B
1. _____	1. _____
2. _____	2. _____
3. _____	3. _____
4. _____	4. _____
5. _____	5. _____

Reflect and Plan: Do you feel closer after learning about each other's fears? What bucket list activity could make you feel even closer or help each other overcome your fears?

Bucket List Item: _____

_____

LONG–DISTANCE LETTERS

Pretend that you and your partner are newly dating each other but one of you has suddenly been called away, so that you are temporarily in a long-distance relationship. You can pretend you've been separated for any reason, drawn from any point in history—one of you must go abroad on a military mission, or on a scientific mission through the jungle or space. Writing letters is your only means of keeping in touch and getting to know each other better.

Write each other letters, telling your partner something about your life that they don't know. Talk about how these experiences have shaped you as a person. Remember, you're trying to get your "new partner" to really know and understand you.

Supplies Needed: Paper, pens or pencils

Reflect and Plan: Can letters or writing be a tool that you can use to become closer and feel more intimate? What are some other ways you can experience intimacy? Did anything in these letters hint at something you would want to try together?

Bucket List Item: _____

_____

_____

WHAT'S THEIR STORY?

Have you ever wondered about the background stories of your favorite fictional characters? Some films and books include that information, but many don't. In this activity, imagine a story from a favorite character's past. What was Jack from *Titanic*'s childhood like? What was it like when Dorothy from *The Wizard of Oz* first adopted Toto? Get creative! You can keep it going and talk about as many different characters as you want.

Vote on your favorite story and write it down here, if you'd like.

_____

_____

_____

_____

_____

_____

_____

_____

_____

_____

_____

_____

_____

Reflect and Plan: What kinds of experiences did these characters have in your stories? Is there anything about how they lived that appeals to you? Would you like to encounter it in your real life?

Bucket List Items: _____

_____

_____

PRESIDENTIAL OPPORTUNITY

Imagine that you had the opportunity to become president of your country. What would you do? There could be many advantages and disadvantages to having that position. Would you like to be the leader and have that much power? If you did accept the opportunity, what kinds of changes would you make to your country? If you could also have an impact on the world, what kinds of things would you try to change? If you didn't accept the opportunity, why wouldn't you do it?

   Talk and write about both the pros and the cons of taking on that kind of power and responsibility.

Partner A: _____

_____

_____

_____

_____

Partner B: _____

_____

_____

_____

_____

Reflect and Plan: Think about the future and what you would like to change in order for the world to be a better place. What can the two of you do to contribute to this?

Bucket List Item: _____

_____

BLIND DATE MATCHMAKING

Think of some single people you and your partner know. After each name, write down their most important qualities—whether they're outgoing, intellectual, scatterbrained, bighearted, or anything else that stands out about them.

Then pretend that you are matchmakers and imagine which friends you would pair up. Ask each other questions such as "What would they like about each other?" "What would they dislike?" "Do you think they would have fun?" "What kind of date would they go on?" or "What would they talk about?"

PARTNER A'S FRIENDS

1. _____

_____

2. _____

_____

3. _____

_____

4. _____

_____

5. _____

_____

PARTNER B'S FRIENDS

1. _____

_____

2. _____

_____

3. _____

_____

4. _____

5. _____

GOOD MATCHES

1. _____

2. _____

3. _____

4. _____

5. _____

Reflect and Plan: What would have happened if you and your partner had met on a blind date? Do you want to role-play and act it out now? If you did meet on a blind date, try to re-create how it went!

Bucket List Item: _____

_____

KNOWING YOUR FUTURE

Many of us would love to know what is going to happen in the future. In fact, there are entire industries built on this desire, such as psychic hotlines and websites.

Would you like to know your future? If so, what would you like to know—good things or bad things? For example, would you like to know the exact date of your death? If you will have a major career change? How rich you will be? Would you opt to know only the good and not the bad? Why do you feel this way? After talking these questions over, have fun and write down some silly or serious predictions for your future.

Partner A: _____

_____

_____

Partner B: _____

_____

_____

Reflect and Plan: Look back at what you wrote down. Is there one thing that stands out to you most? Don't let it just be a speculation. Put it on your bucket list and plan to check it off!

Bucket List Items: _____

_____

_____

SELF-REFLECTION

Every partnership should be based on give and take. But sometimes we get so caught up in our own needs, we forget to meet our partner's.

On separate sheets of paper, take a few minutes to each answer these questions. Over the last 24 hours . . .

* What have I received from my partner?

* What have I given my partner?

* What troubles have I caused them?

* What joy have I brought to them?

Share your answers with each other and discuss them. Reflecting on these questions will help you become closer and happier.

Supplies Needed: Paper, pens or pencils

Reflect and Plan: Ask your partner what you could do for them to make them feel like their needs are being met. You can think big or small.

Bucket List Items: _____

_____

_____

FIRST-IMPRESSION CHANGES

Research shows that people form a first impression within seconds of meeting someone—sometimes, depending on the circumstances, they begin to form that impression before they even meet them. Think back to your first date or first meeting. Try to remember what your first impression was of your now-partner in the following categories as well as your current impression. Add your own categories to the list, if you'd like.

CATEGORY		PARTNER A	PARTNER B
Looks	First impression		
	Current		
Personality	First impression		
	Current		
Intelligence	First impression		
	Current		
Dress/style	First impression		
	Current		
Humor	First impression		
	Current		
Outgoing/shy	First impression		
	Current		
Easy to talk to/or not	First impression		
	Current		

CATEGORY		PARTNER A	PARTNER B
	First impression		
	Current		
	First impression		
	Current		
	First impression		
	Current		
	First impression		
	Current		
	First impression		
	Current		

Reflect and Plan: Talk about whether these first impressions were accurate. If they weren't, were you surprised? Is there a category in which you want to change your first impression?

Bucket List Item: _____

_____

_____

SMALL CELEBRATIONS

Many people celebrate only big occasions like birthdays, anniversaries, and major holidays. But who says you can't celebrate anything on any day? There are so many wonderful things in life that we should salute and honor, so why not celebrate the small things, too?

Write down or talk about the important small things in your lives you tend to overlook daily. They could be something as simple as celebrating that you have a roof over your head or that there are beautiful, sunny days. Or it could be an inside joke or something cute that your kids and/or pets did. Whatever you choose, how can you celebrate it?

Partner A: _____

_____

_____

Partner B: _____

_____

_____

Reflect and Plan: What's a totally new way you could celebrate the little OR big things in your lives?

Bucket List Items: _____

_____

_____

BOOK SWAP

Is there a book or story that has stayed with you, entertained you over and over, or profoundly changed your point of view of the world?

Each partner should tell the other about this favorite book, or write it down if they want—the story line, the characters, the genre (mystery, romance, historical, nonfiction, etc.). Tell your partner why the book impacted you so deeply and why it is meaningful to you. Did you identify with the historical time depicted in it? The plotline? The personalities of the characters?

Partner A: _____

_____

_____

Partner B: _____

_____

_____

Reflect and Plan: How can you bring elements from these books into your lives? It could be travel, food, or another activity.

Bucket List Items: _____

_____

_____

FAVORITE THINGS CHALLENGE

Depending on how long you have known your partner, you might think you already know all their favorite things. But do you really? Here is your chance to find out!

For each category, try to guess your partner's favorite things. If you get it wrong, keep guessing until you get it right. Each time you guess wrong, you get a point. The person with the fewest points (i.e., the person who had to guess the fewest number of times to get a correct answer) at the end of the game wins. Record the correct guesses in the following table.

Here are some categories to start with—you can also add your own:

CATEGORY	PARTNER A	PARTNER B
Fabric		
Hot sauce brand		
Flower		
Guilty pleasure		
Comedian		
Fashion accessory		
Body part		

CATEGORY	PARTNER A	PARTNER B

SCORES

Partner A: _____

Partner B: _____

Reflect and Plan: Discuss why these are your favorite things. What's a new way you can experience some of your favorites again, or incorporate them into your life more?

Bucket List Item: _____

_____

_____

DANCE UP A STORM

Dancing can be fun and romantic. It is a challenging activity that can bring you physically close to your partner or just give you an opportunity to let loose and get creative! In the past, if you wanted to learn some dance routines or styles, you would have to take a class or have someone teach you in person. Now you can just easily look it up online!

For this activity, find some online videos that teach you a dance that you have to do with a partner, such as salsa, line dancing, or the cha-cha. Whatever you choose, you will have fun and be physically closer to your partner. You can also try to challenge yourself to learn a short routine or give the dance a signature flair that represents you two as a couple.

Supplies Needed: Smartphone or computer, internet

Keep a record of your experience here, if you'd like. What genre did you try? Was it fun, difficult, or both?

_____

_____

_____

_____

_____

Reflect and Plan: There are many ways you could incorporate dancing into a bucket list item. Do you want to dance more? Or do you want to watch other people dance? If you are already a skilled dancer, how about choreographing a routine for just you two?

Bucket List Items: _____

_____

_____

UNDERSTANDING OTHERS

Even if you know that everyone is different and feel a lot of empathy for others, it can be tough to imagine what life looks like from another person's perspective.

Talk about what you think people who are very different from you experience every day. Here are some ideas to get you going—you can each write down a few ideas here.

* What would it be like to be born and raised in another country?

* What would it be like to an athlete training for the Olympics?

* What would it be like have studied something or trained in something completely different from your own background?

Partner A: _____

_____

_____

Partner B: _____

_____

_____

Reflect and Plan: How can you explore and understand lives different from your own so you can build empathy?

Bucket List Items: _____

_____

_____

CHANGE HISTORY

Historical stories are part of the fabric of most of our lives. Perhaps there's even an area of history you're especially interested in, like World War I or the Gold Rush era.

In this activity, you're going to take what you know about history and turn it upside down. Think of some historical moments that are especially meaningful to you, and then write a paragraph or talk about what would have happened if those moments had turned out differently. What if the assassin's bullet had missed Lincoln? What if the United States had joined World War II from the very beginning? Imagine how the world would be different.

PARTNER A

1. _____

_____

_____

_____

_____

_____

_____

2. _____

_____

_____

_____

_____

_____

_____

3. _____

_____

_____

_____

_____

_____

PARTNER B

1. _____
   _____
   _____
   _____
   _____
   _____
   _____

2. _____
   _____
   _____
   _____
   _____
   _____
   _____

3. _____
   _____
   _____
   _____
   _____
   _____

Reflect and Plan: What are your favorite stories in history? Are there any associated landmarks or museums that you could plan a visit to?

Bucket List Item: _____
_____
_____

DREAM VACATION

The world is full of places to see and explore—many of them places you may be interested in but don't feel are practical to visit. But finding out where you'd each like to go (even if you don't end up going there) can teach you a lot.

Both partners should write down answers to questions about travel: Where do you want to go? Why do you want to go there? What is the most exciting thing about that place? What are the main attractions/activities you would like to do there? How long would you like to stay?

For this exercise, don't consider practical things like money or time away from work/family. Remember, this is your DREAM vacation—it's about your dreams and desires.

PARTNER A

Where I want to go and why: _____

_____

The most exciting thing about that place: _____

_____

The main attractions or activities I would like to see or do: _____

_____

_____

_____

_____

How long I would like to stay: _____

PARTNER B

Where I want to go and why: _____

_____

The most exciting thing about that place: _____

_____

The main attractions or activities I would like to see or do: _____

_____

_____

_____

_____

How long I would like to stay: _____

Reflect and Plan: Discuss how you could make these a reality someday. Try to be concrete so that you can take action soon.

Bucket List Item: _____

_____

_____

INTUITION

When deciding, some people prefer to use logic and reason over their emotions while others go with their gut feeling rather than think and analyze their decisions too much.

What do you think this gut feeling or intuition really is? Do you think it's more reliable than logic and reason? Have you ever followed this feeling when logic and facts contradict what it is telling you to do? If so, how did it turn out? And if you do not follow it, why not? Are you afraid to do so? If so, what are you afraid of?

Partner A: _____

_____

_____

Partner B: _____

_____

_____

Reflect and Plan: Think back on your life and reflect on the gut feelings you have had in the past. In retrospect, were they steering you in the right direction? What kind of activity could help you make use of your gut instinct?

Bucket List Item: _____

_____

_____

HOW LONG COULD YOU GO ON?

Many of us want to live a life of comfort, with plenty of food, money, clothes, and anything else we want. But have you thought about how long you could last if you were suddenly thrown into some very uncomfortable circumstances?

Ask each other how long you could go on in places such as:

* A submarine near the ocean's floor

* An Antarctic research station

* A cabin on a snowy mountain, miles away from your nearest neighbor

* A country where you don't speak a word of the language

* A rustic house with no indoor plumbing

* A home with 40 dogs, cats, or birds in it

* Complete isolation

These are just a few to get you started. Come up with your own categories, too.

Partner A: _____

_____

_____

Partner B: _____

_____

_____

Reflect and Plan: Discuss why you feel like you could (or could not) handle some of these situations for a long time. Are there any on the list that you can imagine being fun?

Bucket List Item: _____

_____

_____

TIME TRAVEL

What if time travel really existed? What if you had the chance to hop in a vessel that would take you to any point in the past? Or the future? What would you choose, and why?

Each partner should write down where they'd go. Would you go back and witness the Gettysburg Address? See the Egyptians building the pyramids? Meet Gandhi? Where would you go in the future? Would you go within your lifetime, or perhaps thousands of years ahead?

After you write down your past and future destinations, talk to each other about why you chose what you did. What appeals to you about time travel? What would scare you? What would you want to know about the future? How do you think it will be different from present day?

PARTNER A
Past destinations:

1. _____
2. _____
3. _____
4. _____
5. _____

Future destinations:

1. _____
2. _____
3. _____
4. _____
5. _____

PARTNER B
Past destinations:

1. _____
2. _____
3. _____
4. _____
5. _____

Future destinations:

1. _____
2. _____
3. _____
4. _____
5. _____

Reflect and Plan: While you can't actually travel through time, you can visit some historical landmarks. Where would you two most want to visit?

Bucket List Item: _____

_____
_____

LOYALTY AND BOUNDARIES

Many people value loyalty in their lives, but sometimes it can be challenging to be loyal all the time, even to the ones you love. Here is a chance to think about where your boundaries are.

Discuss these scenarios:

* You discovered that your sister was selling classified secrets to your country's enemy. Would you turn her in?

* Your teenage child stole a $100 item from a store. Would you turn them in?

* Your partner embezzled money from their place of employment. Would you turn them in?

Continue to come up with your own scenarios.

Partner A: _____

_____

_____

Partner B: _____

_____

_____

Reflect and Plan: What did you learn about yourself and your partner from this activity? What are some ways that you both can use your loyalty to enhance your lives together?

Bucket List Item: _____

_____

INSPIRING PEOPLE

You probably have a few people who have inspired you in your life—people you knew or only heard of, people who were living or dead. No matter who they were, something about their life or story resonated with you.

This is an opportunity to think back on who inspired you and why. Ask yourself why they inspired you, what you learned from them, and how you became a better person from that lesson.

Next, think about how you yourself may have inspired people in your life. We don't always necessarily know if and when others were inspired by us, but if we look closely, we can probably have a good guess.

PARTNER A

Who inspired you? _____

Whom did you inspire? _____

_____

_____

PARTNER B

Who inspired you? _____

Whom did you inspire? _____

_____

_____

Reflect and Plan: What are some things you can do in the future to keep inspiring others?

Bucket List Item: _____

_____

A LETTER TO YOUR FUTURE SELF

The reality of life is that we all pass on some day—hopefully when we are old and have lived a fulfilling life. But what if you had a chance stay alive forever? What would you want to make sure you always remembered?

Here's the hypothetical: You have the chance to freeze yourself for a certain amount of time that you agree to beforehand—it could be 10 years, 50 years, 100 years, 1,000 years, or longer. After that period of time, you would be unfrozen and resume your life—but you will have forgotten some things about your life and your partner. Write a letter to your future, unfrozen self about the memories you want to rediscover when you resume your life in the far, far future. If comfortable, you can share your letter with your partner.

Supplies Needed: Paper, pens or pencils

Reflect and Plan: Talk about the things that would be different when you are unfrozen. What might the world look like? What kind of technology will exist? Is there anything you'd like to do now that feels futuristic or like it might be around in the distant future?

Bucket List Item: _____

_____

_____

HIDDEN HABITS

Humans are creatures of habit—some of us more than others, but we all have our routines to some extent. Some of these routines are obvious to others; some we keep hidden for one reason or another.

Talk to your partner, or write, about some of the hidden habits you have that your partner doesn't even know about. It could be something like not stepping on sidewalk cracks, counting steps as you go up or down stairs, or that you have coffee at exactly 10:30 every morning at work.

Partner A: _____

_____

_____

Partner B: _____

_____

_____

Reflect and Plan: Talk about where you think these habits came from. Do they bother you? Are you embarrassed? Do they comfort you? Is there anything about them that is fun and exciting that you would like to bring more of into your life?

Bucket List Items: _____

_____

_____

MOVIE REWRITE

Even if you love movies, you have probably seen a few that you wish turned out a bit differently. Each partner should write down at least two of their favorite movies. Then discuss what was good about them and what (if anything) was bad.

Now it's time for a rewrite! What would you change about the movie? The plot? The actors? The ending? How would things go differently for the characters if you made these changes?

PARTNER A

Movie name: _____

Rewrite: _____

_____

_____

_____

_____

_____

_____

Movie name: _____

Rewrite: _____

_____

_____

_____

_____

_____

_____

PARTNER B

Movie name: _____

Rewrite: _____

_____

_____

_____

_____

_____

_____

Movie name: _____

Rewrite: _____

_____

_____

_____

_____

_____

_____

Reflect and Plan: If you're big film fans, research film festivals you could attend. Whether they're nearby or require a trip, it could be an exciting experience!

Bucket List Items: _____

_____

_____

FUNNY PICTURES

If you find that most of the photos of you and your partner are serious, this activity is for you. For this activity, you are going to take as many funny pictures of each other as you can. You could come up with different themes or challenges for the photos. Make sure some are creative, such as dressing your partner up in whatever silly or unusual outfits you want to. Or you could even blindfold them while you get them dressed so they can't see what you put them in before they open their eyes.

Supplies Needed: Smartphone or camera, clothes, accessories/props

Theme ideas or challenges:

1. _____   6. _____

2. _____   7. _____

3. _____   8. _____

4. _____   9. _____

5. _____   10. _____

Reflect and Plan: These photos can help make memories. Where are some places you really want to take photos of? What are things you want to record yourself doing?

Bucket List Items: _____

_____

_____

DESCRIBE IT TO ME

When you describe a place, you likely use a lot of visual imagery—talking about its color, size, or anything else you could see if you were there. But in this activity, you will try to rely on your other senses to help your partner "see" a place.

Each partner should describe a place, either in writing or aloud. It could be anything from a room in your home to a historical landmark. Describe it to your partner using words that support the other senses—taste, touch, smell, or sound only, with no mention of how it looks. See how creative you can get. Then try to guess the place being described.

Supplies Needed: Paper, pens or pencils

Partner A: _____

_____

_____

Partner B: _____

_____

_____

Reflect and Plan: Discuss other ways you could make greater use of your four other senses.

Bucket List Item: _____

_____

_____

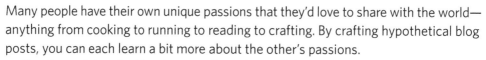

YOUR FIRST BLOG POST

Many people have their own unique passions that they'd love to share with the world—anything from cooking to running to reading to crafting. By crafting hypothetical blog posts, you can each learn a bit more about the other's passions.

For this activity, decide what your hypothetical blog would be about and if you'd like to create one together or separately. Then choose a name for it—it could be related to the topic, an inside joke, whatever you'd like. Write a short blog entry (just a few sentences) that would serve as your introduction to your audience and your topic. Be sure that you write about the importance of the topic, your expertise, and how it will benefit the reader. Then swap "posts" with each other and learn more about your passions!

PARTNER A

My expertise: _____

_____

Topic of choice: _____

_____

Importance of topic: _____

_____

How blog/topic will benefit the reader: _____

_____

Introduction to blog: _____

_____

_____

_____

PARTNER B

My expertise: _____
_____
_____

Topic of choice: _____
_____
_____

Importance of topic: _____
_____
_____

How blog/topic will benefit the reader: _____
_____
_____

Introduction to blog: _____
_____
_____
_____
_____

Reflect and Plan: Will you create this blog for your bucket list item, or does it inspire you to do something else? Discuss how you can incorporate more of the passion you wrote about into your life.

Bucket List Item: _____
_____

CELEBRITY CRUSHES

Many people have had secret, or not so secret, celebrity crushes, whether in the past or present. If you are both comfortable discussing this, talk with your partner about who yours have been through the years. Start with your childhood, then work up to the present day.

Discuss, or write about, why you had these crushes and what it was about these celebrities that made you like them. What would you imagine their real-life personalities to be? Do you think you would like the real person? Do you think they would be very different from their public persona?

Partner A: _____

_____

_____

Partner B: _____

_____

_____

Reflect and Plan: Are there ways you can take some of the qualities that make you like certain celebrities and incorporate them into your life?

Bucket List Items: _____

_____

_____

AT-HOME "PUB CRAWL"

If you used to enjoy pub crawls but no longer feel like you have the time, great news: With a little creativity, you can have fun putting one together at home!

Pick a few different drinks to symbolize different types of bars. Feel free to select nonalcoholic drinks as well. Think up what kinds of beverages you might find in a:

* Beer garden
* Martini bar
* European pub
* Winery
* Juice bar
* Café

Once you've made your picks, set up the supplies you need for the drinks around a room or your home. (You can also decorate the room themed around your favorite bar, if you have the time or inclination.) Then go from spot to spot, making and sipping the drinks, playing some music, and enjoying the experience.

Supplies Needed: Cocktail ingredients, drinking glasses, music

Keep track of your "pubs" and drinks here, if you'd like.

Reflect and Plan: What do the drinks mean to you? Why did you select them? Do they remind you of traveling and trying new things?

Bucket List Items: _____

_____

GREAT INVENTIONS

How many times have you seen a new product or invention come onto the market and thought, *Gosh, I wish I would have thought of that! It's brilliant!* Now is your chance to try your hand at exactly that, by figuring out the next great invention that the world needs.

Each of you should "invent" a new product or service that you think would make your lives (and the world) better. It can be realistic (like a new kind of cell phone holder) or fantastical (a robot massage therapist). Get creative and have fun. Define the invention's purpose, its features, what it would do, who would buy it, how much it would cost, and how you would market it. Draw a quick design for the invention on separate sheets of paper, too.

Supplies Needed: Paper, pens or pencils

PARTNER A

Purpose: _____

_____

Features: _____

_____

What it does: _____

_____

Who would buy it: _____

_____

Price: _____

How to market it: _____

_____

PARTNER B

Purpose: _____

_____

Features: _____

_____

What it does: _____

_____

Who would buy it: _____

_____

Price: _____

How to market it: _____

_____

Reflect and Plan: Since these new inventions are intended to make your lives better, what can you do that will improve your lives right now? Can you create a small invention or new system for your home? It doesn't have to be complicated—it just has to improve your lives, even just a little bit.

Bucket List Item: _____

_____

COUPLE'S MASSAGE

Massages not only feel good, but they are also good for you, relieving tension and lowering stress levels. So why not create a spa in your own home?

Pick out the most relaxing space in your home, and make a specific area—the bed, the floor, the couch—the massage area. Decorate that area with romantic decor such as candles, silk, flowers, and music. Take turns giving and receiving the massage, making sure to ask questions about where and how they'd like to be massaged.

You might even want to get more adventurous and add some sensual items (such as edible massage oil) into the massage to spice it up.

Supplies Needed: Candles, massage oil, flowers, blanket, music

Keep a record of your experience here, if you'd like. Did the massage help you feel physically closer to your partner?

_____

_____

_____

_____

Reflect and Plan: Think about a kind of self-care you've always wanted to try. Have you not been able to find the time to make it happen? What do you need to do to feel like you can take time for yourself?

Bucket List Items: _____

_____

DREAM CAREER

Some people spend their childhoods dreaming about what they would like to do for work as an adult. Maybe for you it was being a movie star, an NBA player, or the next Oprah Winfrey.

   Discuss your childhood dream professions with your partner. Also feel free to write them down. Then talk about what industries you would find it most exciting to work in now. Do you want to be famous? What would you choose if you thought you could do it? Don't worry about the limitations (such as being an NBA player if you are only five-foot-seven). The point of this discussion is to explore your values and interests and understand why your partner has these dreams.

Partner A: _____

_____

_____

Partner B: _____

_____

_____

Reflect and Plan: Think about how you could incorporate some of these values and interests into your future. It doesn't have to be a full career change—small changes that connect you to your dream, just for the fun of it, are also great.

Bucket List Items: _____

_____

_____

ON THE AIR

Have a conversation and record it! Start your own couple's podcast and show off the chemistry you have with each other. Record your pilot episode about anything you want to talk about. Choose a topic and the name of your podcast, and consider the format and length. Do you want it to be a Q and A podcast? Or storytelling? Maybe you would invite guests such as your friends or even your kids, if you have any. Hit "Record" on your phone or voice recorder and that's it. You have your pilot! If you like what you have, consider getting a podcast-editing app and audio file host to prep your show for upload onto the internet.

Supplies Needed: Smartphone (or voice recorder), internet

Topic: _____

_____

_____

_____

Name: _____

Format: _____

_____

_____

_____

Episode summary: _____

_____

_____

_____

Additional notes: _____

_____

_____

_____

_____

_____

_____

_____

_____

_____

_____

_____

_____

_____

_____

_____

_____

_____

_____

_____

Reflect and Plan: The activity itself might be a bucket list item for you, but maybe it can also inspire you to do something similar. What other activities show off your chemistry? Get your creative juices going!

Bucket List Items: _____

_____

_____

EXTREMES

How well do you handle extremes? For example, how long could you go without talking? How high could you climb before you started feeling scared? Write down different categories (sports, heights, sleep, work, etc.) and whether you can handle extremes in that area of life.

Next, discuss your feelings around these extremes. Which would be the most difficult for you to handle? Are there any situations where you might find a safe extreme to be an enjoyable experience? Why or why not?

PARTNER A

1.

2.

3.

4.

5.

PARTNER B

1. _____
   _____
   _____

2. _____
   _____
   _____

3. _____
   _____
   _____

4. _____
   _____
   _____

5. _____
   _____
   _____

Reflect and Plan: Think about whether there are any safe extreme activities that you would like to try. There are plenty in the world—it just depends on how far you want to push yourself!

Bucket List Items: _____

_____

_____

PERFECT PARTY GUESTS

Whom do you admire? The answer may include anyone from people you know well, such as your parents, to historical figures such as Michelangelo, Van Gogh, or Mother Teresa. Whomever you admire, imagine what it would be like to invite them to a party at your home.

Write down at least five different admired party guests each. Try to mix it up between people you know and people who are outside your immediate life. What would you talk about with each of the guests? Would you invite them all together or meet up with each one separately? Would you and your partner enjoy similar parties? Or vastly different ones?

PARTNER A	PARTNER B
1. _____	1. _____
2. _____	2. _____
3. _____	3. _____
4. _____	4. _____
5. _____	5. _____

Reflect and Plan: Discuss why you chose these particular people for your party. Which of their qualities do you admire and why? What did they accomplish in life that you would like to do yourself?

Bucket List Items: _____

_____

_____

CHOICES

Even if we try to make good choices, many of us have had some not-so-proud moments in life.

For example, there are plenty of people who cheated on tests in school while growing up. There are many reasons people cheat, but the bottom line is that they cheat to get something they want.

Did you ever cheat on a test when you were young? Did your partner? If so, what did you cheat on and why? If you haven't cheated on anything, can you ever imagine a scenario in life where you would cheat to get some sort of benefit? Would you cheat at work? Or on your taxes? Or in any other scenario? If so, what would it be and why? If not, why wouldn't you?

Partner A: _____

_____

_____

Partner B: _____

_____

_____

Reflect and Plan: What are the things you want so badly in life that you would be willing to cheat if you couldn't get caught? For your bucket list, think about how you could achieve or obtain these things without cheating.

Bucket List Items: _____

_____

_____

THE FUTURE

What will the future be like? Will the world be better or worse in 100 years? What about in 1,000 years? How will human society and the natural world have changed? Each partner should write down what they think will change in 100, 1,000, and 10,000 years, and then discuss their answers.

PARTNER A

100 years: _____

_____

_____

_____

_____

_____

_____

1,000 years: _____

_____

_____

_____

_____

_____

_____

10,000 years: _____

_____

_____

_____

_____

_____

_____

PARTNER B

100 years: _____

_____

_____

_____

_____

_____

1,000 years: _____

_____

_____

_____

_____

_____

_____

10,000 years: _____

_____

_____

_____

_____

_____

_____

Reflect and Plan: How can you use some of these ideas
to make your own mark on the world?

Bucket List Items: _____

_____

_____

HONEST PERCEPTIONS

We all have our impressions and perceptions of other people. Some of them are good, and some are bad. But have you ever wondered what people's impressions of you are?

Sure, for better or worse, some people have told us what they think of us. But most people keep these kinds of opinions to themselves. So, if you could, would you want to know everyone's honest perception of you? Why or why not? Would you want to hear only the good and not the bad? What if hearing the bad things would help you become a better person?

Partner A: _____

_____

_____

Partner B: _____

_____

_____

Reflect and Plan: There are always things that people would like to change about themselves. Is there anything you would like to change so you could be the best version of yourself? What would you change?

Bucket List Items: _____

_____

_____

CHANGED CHILDHOOD

Everyone has a unique childhood. From the kinds of parents and siblings you had to the experiences you had in school—they are all memorable. But is there anything you would change?

For example, would you have your parents or guardians be more or less strict? Would you have preferred to go on more vacations or fewer? Would you have liked more or fewer siblings? Would you have liked to attend a different school? Think about anything that you might want to change. Even if you wouldn't change a thing, how would your life have turned out differently if you did change something?

Partner A: _____

_____

_____

Partner B: _____

_____

_____

Reflect and Plan: Is there something that you always wanted to do during your childhood but never got the chance? How can you do it now, together?

Bucket List Items: _____

_____

_____

CUTE CARICATURES

You may have gotten a caricature done before at a party or fair—they tend to exaggerate and simplify your characteristics. In this exercise, each partner should draw a caricature of their favorite qualities about the other. For example, if you love your partner's eyebrows, you can draw them as bigger than their head; if you love their musical ability, you can draw them performing on guitar in front of a stadium of fans. This activity is not a contest—it's simply for fun and to remind each other how much you love the other's qualities!

If you're artistically inclined, you can try something more advanced than just pen and paper, and experiment with paint or charcoal.

Supplies Needed: Your choice of art supplies: Paper, pencils, canvas, paintbrushes, paint, markers, charcoal, clay (if you prefer to sculpt)

PARTNER A

PARTNER B

Reflect and Plan: Is there a museum you've always wanted to visit or an art project you've wanted to try? How about body art? What new, exciting activity can you do that involves art?

Bucket List Item: _____

_____

_____

LOST AND FOUND

Whether you've experienced only a small loss, such as the loss of a beloved family heirloom, or dealt with a major loss, such as the loss of a loved one, loss is a part of all our lives. This activity is a chance to reflect on objects, people, or experiences that you have lost in your life.

Loss is subjective. For example, a person doesn't need to be dead for them to be lost from your life. Loss also doesn't have to be negative—maybe you lost a job, and this changed your life for the better. So, think about your losses and how they have changed you. Did they make your life better or worse? Did the loss change you as a person? If so, how?

Partner A: _____

_____

_____

Partner B: _____

_____

_____

Reflect and Plan: What are some positive losses you have experienced (e.g., loss of a phobia, gotten rid of bad habits)? What are some activities those losses could inspire?

Bucket List Items: _____

_____

_____

WHAT WOULD YOU DO?

Let's suppose that you are out at a restaurant or a mall, minding your own business, when you see a good friend of yours, who you know is in a monogamous relationship, holding hands with a person who is not their spouse. They are clearly romantically involved, which means your friend is cheating.

What would you do? Would you pretend you didn't see it and not say anything? Would you confront your friend? Would you tell your friend's spouse that you found out they were cheating? Why would you make whatever choice you did?

Partner A: _____

_____

_____

Partner B: _____

_____

_____

Reflect and Plan: Some people do things that are considered scandalous or that are unethical, such as cheating, even though they know it hurts people, because they like the excitement. What exciting, "scandalous" things can you do with your partner that are *not* unethical and wouldn't hurt anyone?

Bucket List Items: _____

_____

_____

REEL CHALLENGE

Plan a long evening together where you each choose a movie to watch together. It could be one of your favorites or one chosen at random. Watch each movie, and when it ends, both of you write down your top five favorite scenes.

Next, play a guessing game. Ask your partner to name at least two or three scenes that they thought were your favorites and have them explain why they think you liked them. See who has the most accurate guesses.

Supplies Needed: Pens or pencils; paper; DVD, streaming service, or TV channel

SCORES:

Partner A: _____

Partner B: _____

Reflect and Plan: Talk about why you liked or didn't like these scenes. Do they represent something bigger for you? What was exciting about them? Pick one of the scenes and figure out how you can turn it into a bucket list item.

Bucket List Item: _____

_____

_____

ADVENTURE OR SECURITY?

Everyone is wired differently. Some people crave a good adrenaline rush while others spend most of their lives avoiding it and seeking comfort in routine.

So, which do you prefer? Would you rather live a life of wild turbulence, with highs and lows, successes and failures, and lots of passion and adventure? Or would you rather live a life of predictability, security, and ease? Why do you feel that way?

Partner A: _____

_____

_____

Partner B: _____

_____

_____

Reflect and Plan: What are some wild, adventurous things that you could do together that feel fun for both of you? How can you and your partner find a middle ground between adventure and security?

Bucket List Items: _____

_____

_____

TIME MACHINE AND FUTURE SELF

Pretend that you are much older and reflecting on your life. What did your younger self do? What advice would you give them now if you could? You may just want to congratulate or comfort your younger self.

Partner A: _____

_____

_____

Partner B: _____

_____

_____

Reflect and Plan: Think about the advice you would give your younger self and then consider the parts of your life that haven't happened yet. What can you do to keep yourself from feeling regret when you get older?

Bucket List Items: _____

_____

_____

SACRIFICE FOR HUMANITY

Would you love to have world peace? Or cure all the major diseases? Or put an end to world hunger? Of course you would—most of us wish the world were a happier, healthier place.

Imagine a scenario where you could achieve all these goals! Sounds great, right? But not so fast! What if someone made you an offer that if you sacrificed yourself in some way, the rest of the world could live in bliss? How far would you go? Would you be willing to be locked inside your home forever? Never get on the internet ever again?

Partner A: _____

_____

_____

Partner B: _____

_____

_____

Reflect and Plan: Talk about what you would be giving up with your sacrifice. How much would you miss it? Are there any important sacrifices you would like to incorporate into your life right now?

Bucket List Item: _____

_____

_____

YOUR LEGACY

While we are going about our daily lives, we might not really think about what the world would be like after we're gone. But what will your legacy be? What would you like your children and grandchildren or other people who will come after you to say about you? What would you like to teach other people? What kind of positive impact would you like to have on society as a whole? Talk with your partner about the kind of legacy you'd like to leave and write down some ideas.

Partner A: _____

_____

_____

Partner B: _____

_____

_____

Reflect and Plan: You don't have to wait to do these things. You can start creating your legacy today, doing things to make your mark on the world. Brainstorm some ways you can begin to take action.

Bucket List Items: _____

_____

_____

FASHION SHOW

Many of us have more clothes than we actually need. In fact, there may even be clothes in your closets that you have forgotten about. Now is the time to rediscover them!

Take turns trying on old clothes and modeling them for your partner. Create new outfits, sexy or serious, that you might actually want to wear out of the house someday. Get as creative as you can with accessories such as jewelry, shoes, hats, etc.

Supplies Needed: Old clothes, shoes, accessories such as scarves, hats, or jewelry

Keep a record of your experience here, if you'd like. Did you have any favorite outfits?

_____

_____

_____

_____

_____

Reflect and Plan: Are there any dream shopping trips you've always wanted to take? Think about different cities or even countries.

Bucket List Items: _____

_____

_____

A MESSAGE FOR YOU

In this activity, you will write a message for your partner—on their back! While one partner stands or sits facing away from the other partner with their back to them, the other partner uses their finger to write a message on the partner's back, one letter at a time. Make sure to write large letters so it will be a little easier for your partner to decipher. The partner who is facing away will write down the message they think they received and see if they got it right. Take turns doing this and experiment with different kinds of messages, from something funny to maybe even something a little sexy. You can write down the messages here after for memory keeping.

PARTNER A'S MESSAGES

1. _____

2. _____

3. _____

4. _____

5. _____

PARTNER B'S MESSAGES

1. _____
   _____
   _____

2. _____
   _____
   _____

3. _____
   _____
   _____

4. _____
   _____
   _____

5. _____
   _____
   _____

Reflect and Plan: Many times, we are so focused on our senses of vision, hearing, smell, and taste that we don't pay much attention to our sense of touch. What can you do to incorporate enjoying touch together as a couple?

Bucket List Item: _____
_____
_____

CREATE YOUR OWN PUZZLE

Though it's easy to find a wide variety of puzzles at the store, a puzzle you and your partner make together will have more meaning and can become a cherished possession.

First, get a piece of thick paper, poster board, or construction paper. Decide what you want to draw. Both of you should help create the art—if one of you is a better visual artist, they can draw while the other colors. Then flip the paper over and draw puzzle piece shapes. If you're not sure what shapes to draw, you can find puzzle piece patterns online.

Cut the paper up into these puzzle pieces. Now it's time for you to solve your very own puzzle!

Supplies Needed: Paper (poster board, construction paper), crayons or markers, scissors

Keep a record of your experience here, if you'd like. What did you end up drawing for your puzzle?

_____

_____

_____

_____

_____

Reflect and Plan: Do you like puzzles? Is it the mental challenge? Is it relaxing? Are there other activities similar to completing a puzzle that you'd like to try?

Bucket List Items: _____

_____

WHAT'S YOUR HOBBY?

Perhaps you already know each other's hobbies. Maybe there are some you don't know about. Either way, select one of your partner's hobbies to try. Help each other gather the materials or supplies needed for the hobbies.

You can do the separate hobbies side by side or do each one together, taking time to teach each other. As you work on the hobby, one partner can talk about why they like it, how it makes them feel, and how it feels to share it with their partner. The other partner trying out the hobby for the first time can express how the hobby feels to them and how it feels to share the experience with their partner.

Supplies Needed: Whatever the hobbies require

Keep a record of your discussion here, if you'd like. How did it feel to share the hobbies together?

_____

_____

_____

_____

_____

_____

Reflect and Plan: Are the hobbies something you want to keep doing together? Or is there something you both haven't tried before but want to try out together?

Bucket List Item: _____

_____

_____

LOVE LANGUAGE

Learn to say "I love you" in 10 languages! And to make each utterance more meaningful, add "You make me feel happy" as well. Or maybe you just want to say "I like you!" or you have a special phrase just between yourselves. Use a website or app to look up lists of languages and to translate these phrases. You can even come up with your own list of languages from the places you want to travel to together or that you have always wanted to learn.

Supplies Needed: Smartphone or computer, internet

LANGUAGE: _____

"I love you": _____

Special phrase: _____

LANGUAGE: _____

"I love you": _____

Special phrase: _____

LANGUAGE: _____

"I love you": _____

Special phrase: _____

LANGUAGE: _____

"I love you": _____

Special phrase: _____

LANGUAGE: _____

"I love you": _____

Special phrase: _____

LANGUAGE: _____

"I love you": _____

Special phrase: _____

LANGUAGE: _____

"I love you": _____

Special phrase: _____

LANGUAGE: _____

"I love you": _____

Special phrase: _____

LANGUAGE: _____

"I love you": _____

Special phrase: _____

LANGUAGE: _____

"I love you": _____

Special phrase: _____

Reflect and Plan: Different cultures around the world express love differently. Think about how you can explore these unique ways you can love each other in a way that is not the same as you do now.

Bucket List Items: _____

_____

_____

CHART THE STARS

If you've ever dreamed about traveling to the stars or spending the entire night out under them, wouldn't it be great if you knew the stories behind them? List a few constellations you'd like to learn more about. Ask your partner to select one from your list and research it. After 15 to 30 minutes, share with each other what you have learned.

Supplies Needed: Smartphone or computer, internet

PARTNER A'S CONSTELLATIONS

1. _____
2. _____
3. _____
4. _____
5. _____

PARTNER B'S CONSTELLATIONS

1. _____
2. _____
3. _____
4. _____
5. _____

Reflect and Plan: Did learning more about the stars make you want to continue to find out more? Did you learn anything interesting? What can you do together to pursue this burgeoning interest in the stars or get closer to them?

Bucket List Items: _____

_____

_____

YOUR MOVIE SOUNDTRACK

You may watch some movies and not even notice the soundtrack. But odds are high that there is at least one film whose soundtrack made a real impression on you, helping set the mood, develop a character, or set the movie's pace.

For this activity, go on the internet or through your personal movie collection and choose 10 songs, each from a different popular movie. Play them for your partner and have them try to guess which movie each is from.

Supplies Needed: Smartphone or computer, internet

Keep a record of your discussion here, if you'd like. Did you notice any similarities or differences in the types of music you each picked?

_____

_____

_____

_____

_____

Reflect and Plan: What did you like best about the music and/or the movie it came from? What bucket list activities do you think the song would be a good soundtrack to?

Bucket List Item: _____

_____

_____

PERFECTLY YOU

Everyone has their own unique blend of personality characteristics. These characteristics are part of why you fell in love with your partner. They may include introversion, extroversion, assertiveness, a sense of humor, nurturing qualities, and much more.

But believe it or not, your partner may not know that you admire certain personality characteristics of theirs, so now is the chance to let them know! Each partner should take some time to reflect on the other's unique blend of personality characteristics and rediscover the magic of why you came together in the first place.

PARTNER A
What I love about Partner B:

1. _____

_____

2. _____

_____

3. _____

_____

4. _____

_____

5. _____

_____

PARTNER B
What I love about Partner A:

1. _____

_____

2. _____

_____

3. _____

_____

4. _____

_____

5. _____

_____

Reflect and Plan: Reflect on how you celebrate what you admire about each other.

Bucket List Item: _____

_____

_____

FAMOUS–COUPLES BINGO

If you haven't played bingo in a while, it's simple: Each player gets a scorecard with the word "BINGO" written across the top and random numbers in each square. The players then listen to the bingo caller, who call outs numbers, with the goal of matching five of the squares in a vertical, horizontal, or diagonal row. The winner calls out "Bingo!"

This activity uses the same basic rules but adapts them for "famous-couples bingo." First, make two bingo cards by drawing a five-by-five-square box on a piece of paper. Fill in the squares of each of your cards with one-half of a famous couple. For example, Tom Hanks and Rita Wilson, Blake Shelton and Gwen Stefani, or Lucille Ball and Desi Arnaz. Each square should have one name. Make sure that each card is different, and fill in every square on both cards.

Then write the names of each person included on the cards on small pieces of paper. Take turns pulling out names and calling them out, until one of you shouts "Bingo!"

Supplies Needed: Paper, pens or pencils

Reflect and Plan: What do you enjoy or not enjoy about games such as bingo? Do you like that it's a chance game, or do you prefer games that require skill?

Bucket List Item: _____

_____

_____

ICING ON THE CAKE

Some things are better said as icing. Become bakers for a day, and make cakes for your partner with special messages. Find an easy cake recipe online or purchase a cake mix; just make sure there are instructions and materials for the icing that you will use for lettering. Then just have fun baking cakes together, getting messy and maybe a little touchy. As the finishing touch, write a special message on each of your cakes for your partner. The message can be funny or serious, but it will always be sweet!

Supplies Needed: Smartphone or computer, internet, cake and icing supplies

Partner A.:'s message: _____

Partner B.:'s message: _____

Reflect and Plan: Whatever activity you want to try together, consider saying a message for your partner as you do it. It could be yelling "I love you" as you bungee jump or just whispering the number of ways your partner inspires you as you watch the sunrise.

Bucket List Items: _____

_____

_____

CHILDHOOD QUESTIONS

For children, the world is endlessly fascinating and beautiful. This is why so many of them seem to go through a phase where, immensely curious about the world and eager to absorb new knowledge, they ask nearly endless questions of any adult they can find. While these questions seem silly now, they also represent an open mind that many of us struggle to connect with in adulthood.

This is an opportunity to revisit and remember all those questions you asked in your childhood, such as "Why don't people on the other side of the world fall off?" or "Does everyone see the color blue the same way?"

Take some time to walk down memory lane and remember what it was like to be a child and that filled with curiosity. If your parents are available, you may even want to call them to help you jog your memory. Then reflect on how you would now answer those questions you still don't have answers to.

PARTNER A'S CHILDHOOD QUESTIONS

1. _____

_____

2. _____

_____

3. _____

_____

4. _____

_____

5. _____

_____

PARTNER B'S CHILDHOOD QUESTIONS

1. _____
   _____

2. _____
   _____

3. _____
   _____

4. _____
   _____

5. _____
   _____

Reflect and Plan: What kinds of activities might help engage your curiosity? Are there any questions you want to try to answer now?

Bucket List Item: _____
_____
_____

MAKE ME LAUGH

Laughter really can be the best medicine. And making someone you love laugh can feel amazing and intimate.

In this activity, you'll each try to come up with some jokes to tell each other. Don't worry if you don't think of yourself as a funny person—no one ever has to hear these jokes except your partner.

Start by choosing a topic area, such as "things that you don't understand." Think about as many things as you can that you find hard to understand in your daily life encounters. Then write a few jokes. You can simply read them to each other or perform them as a comedy routine in your living room.

Partner A: _____

_____

_____

_____

_____

_____

_____

Partner B: _____

_____

_____

_____

_____

_____

_____

Reflect and Plan: What are some ways you can inject more laughter and humor into your relationship?

Bucket List Item: _____

_____

_____

IF I WERE AN ANIMAL

Have you ever identified with an animal? Have you felt lethargic like a sloth, hyper like a bunny, or alpha like a lion? Or maybe you admired a characteristic, such as the cheetah's speed, the bird's flight, or the salmon's ability to swim back to its birthplace no matter how far it has traveled away.

For this prompt, think about what kind of animal you would become if you had to choose. Write down at least five different animals, then talk about why you chose each one.

PARTNER A	PARTNER B
1. _____	1. _____
2. _____	2. _____
3. _____	3. _____
4. _____	4. _____
5. _____	5. _____

Reflect and Plan: If you are animal lovers, how could you incorporate animals into bucket list activities?

Bucket List Items: _____

_____

_____

PART 2

OUR BUCKET LIST

In this part, you'll find the "Master Bucket List and Tracker" to help you record and take action on your bucket list items. Having fun and engaging with each other via the prompts and activities in this book is only the first step to building and strengthening your relationship. Now it's time to make sure that you follow through.

To use the tracker, begin by writing down the bucket list goal that you both created from a prompt or activity. There are extra lines for additional goals in case you had more than one idea from each. Then come up with a target completion date. This is important so you don't forget about doing it. You should even go so far as to put it on your own calendar so it doesn't slip your mind.

Next, write down the page number of the prompt or activity that helped you create the bucket list item. When you have completed the bucket list activity, check the box.

The final step is for you and your partner to write down your favorite memories of the experience. That way, as the years go by, you can look back, talk, and remember the fun you had together!

BUCKET LIST GOAL   Target Complete Date   Page #   Completed

_____   _____   _____   ☐

Partner A's Favorite Memory: _____

Partner B's Favorite Memory: _____

BUCKET LIST GOAL   Target Complete Date   Page #   Completed

_____   _____   _____   ☐

Partner A's Favorite Memory: _____

Partner B's Favorite Memory: _____

BUCKET LIST GOAL   Target Complete Date   Page #   Completed

_____   _____   _____   ☐

Partner A's Favorite Memory: _____

Partner B's Favorite Memory: _____

BUCKET LIST GOAL   Target Complete Date   Page #   Completed

_____   _____   _____   ☐

Partner A's Favorite Memory: _____

Partner B's Favorite Memory: _____

BUCKET LIST GOAL   Target Complete Date   Page #   Completed

_____   _____   _____   ☐

Partner A's Favorite Memory: _____

Partner B's Favorite Memory: _____

BUCKET LIST GOAL   Target Complete Date   Page #   Completed

_____   _____   _____   ☐

Partner A's Favorite Memory: _____

Partner B's Favorite Memory: _____

BUCKET LIST GOAL   Target Complete Date   Page #   Completed

_____   _____   _____   ☐

Partner A's Favorite Memory: _____

Partner B's Favorite Memory: _____

BUCKET LIST GOAL   **Target Complete Date**   **Page #**   **Completed** ☐

Partner A's Favorite Memory: _____

Partner B's Favorite Memory: _____

BUCKET LIST GOAL   **Target Complete Date**   **Page #**   **Completed** ☐

Partner A's Favorite Memory: _____

Partner B's Favorite Memory: _____

BUCKET LIST GOAL   **Target Complete Date**   **Page #**   **Completed** ☐

Partner A's Favorite Memory: _____

Partner B's Favorite Memory: _____

BUCKET LIST GOAL   **Target Complete Date**   **Page #**   **Completed** ☐

Partner A's Favorite Memory: _____

Partner B's Favorite Memory: _____

BUCKET LIST GOAL   **Target Complete Date**   **Page #**   **Completed** ☐

Partner A's Favorite Memory: _____

Partner B's Favorite Memory: _____

BUCKET LIST GOAL   **Target Complete Date**   **Page #**   **Completed** ☐

Partner A's Favorite Memory: _____

Partner B's Favorite Memory: _____

BUCKET LIST GOAL   **Target Complete Date**   **Page #**   **Completed** ☐

Partner A's Favorite Memory: _____

Partner B's Favorite Memory: _____

BUCKET LIST GOAL Target Complete Date Page # Completed

_____ _____ _____ ☐

Partner A's Favorite Memory: _____

Partner B's Favorite Memory: _____

BUCKET LIST GOAL Target Complete Date Page # Completed

_____ _____ _____ ☐

Partner A's Favorite Memory: _____

Partner B's Favorite Memory: _____

BUCKET LIST GOAL Target Complete Date Page # Completed

_____ _____ _____ ☐

Partner A's Favorite Memory: _____

Partner B's Favorite Memory: _____

BUCKET LIST GOAL Target Complete Date Page # Completed

_____ _____ _____ ☐

Partner A's Favorite Memory: _____

Partner B's Favorite Memory: _____

BUCKET LIST GOAL Target Complete Date Page # Completed

_____ _____ _____ ☐

Partner A's Favorite Memory: _____

Partner B's Favorite Memory: _____

BUCKET LIST GOAL Target Complete Date Page # Completed

_____ _____ _____ ☐

Partner A's Favorite Memory: _____

Partner B's Favorite Memory: _____

BUCKET LIST GOAL Target Complete Date Page # Completed

_____ _____ _____ ☐

Partner A's Favorite Memory: _____

Partner B's Favorite Memory: _____

BUCKET LIST GOAL   **Target Complete Date**   **Page #**   **Completed**

_____   _____   _____   ☐

Partner A's Favorite Memory: _____

Partner B's Favorite Memory: _____

BUCKET LIST GOAL   **Target Complete Date**   **Page #**   **Completed**

_____   _____   _____   ☐

Partner A's Favorite Memory: _____

Partner B's Favorite Memory: _____

BUCKET LIST GOAL   **Target Complete Date**   **Page #**   **Completed**

_____   _____   _____   ☐

Partner A's Favorite Memory: _____

Partner B's Favorite Memory: _____

BUCKET LIST GOAL   **Target Complete Date**   **Page #**   **Completed**

_____   _____   _____   ☐

Partner A's Favorite Memory: _____

Partner B's Favorite Memory: _____

BUCKET LIST GOAL   **Target Complete Date**   **Page #**   **Completed**

_____   _____   _____   ☐

Partner A's Favorite Memory: _____

Partner B's Favorite Memory: _____

BUCKET LIST GOAL   **Target Complete Date**   **Page #**   **Completed**

_____   _____   _____   ☐

Partner A's Favorite Memory: _____

Partner B's Favorite Memory: _____

BUCKET LIST GOAL   **Target Complete Date**   **Page #**   **Completed**

_____   _____   _____   ☐

Partner A's Favorite Memory: _____

Partner B's Favorite Memory: _____

BUCKET LIST GOAL Target Complete Date Page # Completed

_____ _____ _____ ☐

Partner A's Favorite Memory: _____

Partner B's Favorite Memory: _____

BUCKET LIST GOAL Target Complete Date Page # Completed

_____ _____ _____ ☐

Partner A's Favorite Memory: _____

Partner B's Favorite Memory: _____

BUCKET LIST GOAL Target Complete Date Page # Completed

_____ _____ _____ ☐

Partner A's Favorite Memory: _____

Partner B's Favorite Memory: _____

BUCKET LIST GOAL Target Complete Date Page # Completed

_____ _____ _____ ☐

Partner A's Favorite Memory: _____

Partner B's Favorite Memory: _____

BUCKET LIST GOAL Target Complete Date Page # Completed

_____ _____ _____ ☐

Partner A's Favorite Memory: _____

Partner B's Favorite Memory: _____

BUCKET LIST GOAL Target Complete Date Page # Completed

_____ _____ _____ ☐

Partner A's Favorite Memory: _____

Partner B's Favorite Memory: _____

BUCKET LIST GOAL Target Complete Date Page # Completed

_____ _____ _____ ☐

Partner A's Favorite Memory: _____

Partner B's Favorite Memory: _____

BUCKET LIST GOAL **Target Complete Date** **Page #** **Completed** ☐

Partner A's Favorite Memory: _____

Partner B's Favorite Memory: _____

BUCKET LIST GOAL **Target Complete Date** **Page #** **Completed** ☐

Partner A's Favorite Memory: _____

Partner B's Favorite Memory: _____

BUCKET LIST GOAL **Target Complete Date** **Page #** **Completed** ☐

Partner A's Favorite Memory: _____

Partner B's Favorite Memory: _____

BUCKET LIST GOAL **Target Complete Date** **Page #** **Completed** ☐

Partner A's Favorite Memory: _____

Partner B's Favorite Memory: _____

BUCKET LIST GOAL **Target Complete Date** **Page #** **Completed** ☐

Partner A's Favorite Memory: _____

Partner B's Favorite Memory: _____

BUCKET LIST GOAL **Target Complete Date** **Page #** **Completed** ☐

Partner A's Favorite Memory: _____

Partner B's Favorite Memory: _____

BUCKET LIST GOAL **Target Complete Date** **Page #** **Completed** ☐

Partner A's Favorite Memory: _____

Partner B's Favorite Memory: _____

BUCKET LIST GOAL Target Complete Date Page # Completed

_____ _____ _____ ☐

Partner A's Favorite Memory: _____
Partner B's Favorite Memory: _____

BUCKET LIST GOAL Target Complete Date Page # Completed

_____ _____ _____ ☐

Partner A's Favorite Memory: _____
Partner B's Favorite Memory: _____

BUCKET LIST GOAL Target Complete Date Page # Completed

_____ _____ _____ ☐

Partner A's Favorite Memory: _____
Partner B's Favorite Memory: _____

BUCKET LIST GOAL Target Complete Date Page # Completed

_____ _____ _____ ☐

Partner A's Favorite Memory: _____
Partner B's Favorite Memory: _____

BUCKET LIST GOAL Target Complete Date Page # Completed

_____ _____ _____ ☐

Partner A's Favorite Memory: _____
Partner B's Favorite Memory: _____

BUCKET LIST GOAL Target Complete Date Page # Completed

_____ _____ _____ ☐

Partner A's Favorite Memory: _____
Partner B's Favorite Memory: _____

BUCKET LIST GOAL Target Complete Date Page # Completed

_____ _____ _____ ☐

Partner A's Favorite Memory: _____
Partner B's Favorite Memory: _____

BUCKET LIST GOAL   **Target Complete Date**   **Page #**   **Completed**   ☐

Partner A's Favorite Memory: _____

Partner B's Favorite Memory: _____

BUCKET LIST GOAL   **Target Complete Date**   **Page #**   **Completed**   ☐

Partner A's Favorite Memory: _____

Partner B's Favorite Memory: _____

BUCKET LIST GOAL   **Target Complete Date**   **Page #**   **Completed**   ☐

Partner A's Favorite Memory: _____

Partner B's Favorite Memory: _____

BUCKET LIST GOAL   **Target Complete Date**   **Page #**   **Completed**   ☐

Partner A's Favorite Memory: _____

Partner B's Favorite Memory: _____

BUCKET LIST GOAL   **Target Complete Date**   **Page #**   **Completed**   ☐

Partner A's Favorite Memory: _____

Partner B's Favorite Memory: _____

BUCKET LIST GOAL   **Target Complete Date**   **Page #**   **Completed**   ☐

Partner A's Favorite Memory: _____

Partner B's Favorite Memory: _____

BUCKET LIST GOAL   **Target Complete Date**   **Page #**   **Completed**   ☐

Partner A's Favorite Memory: _____

Partner B's Favorite Memory: _____

BUCKET LIST GOAL   **Target Complete Date**   **Page #**   **Completed**

⬜

Partner A's Favorite Memory: _____

Partner B's Favorite Memory: _____

BUCKET LIST GOAL   **Target Complete Date**   **Page #**   **Completed**

⬜

Partner A's Favorite Memory: _____

Partner B's Favorite Memory: _____

BUCKET LIST GOAL   **Target Complete Date**   **Page #**   **Completed**

⬜

Partner A's Favorite Memory: _____

Partner B's Favorite Memory: _____

BUCKET LIST GOAL   **Target Complete Date**   **Page #**   **Completed**

⬜

Partner A's Favorite Memory: _____

Partner B's Favorite Memory: _____

BUCKET LIST GOAL   **Target Complete Date**   **Page #**   **Completed**

⬜

Partner A's Favorite Memory: _____

Partner B's Favorite Memory: _____

BUCKET LIST GOAL   **Target Complete Date**   **Page #**   **Completed**

⬜

Partner A's Favorite Memory: _____

Partner B's Favorite Memory: _____

BUCKET LIST GOAL   **Target Complete Date**   **Page #**   **Completed**

⬜

Partner A's Favorite Memory: _____

Partner B's Favorite Memory: _____

BUCKET LIST GOAL   Target Complete Date   Page #   Completed
_____   _____   _____   ☐
Partner A's Favorite Memory: _____
Partner B's Favorite Memory: _____

BUCKET LIST GOAL   Target Complete Date   Page #   Completed
_____   _____   _____   ☐
Partner A's Favorite Memory: _____
Partner B's Favorite Memory: _____

BUCKET LIST GOAL   Target Complete Date   Page #   Completed
_____   _____   _____   ☐
Partner A's Favorite Memory: _____
Partner B's Favorite Memory: _____

BUCKET LIST GOAL   Target Complete Date   Page #   Completed
_____   _____   _____   ☐
Partner A's Favorite Memory: _____
Partner B's Favorite Memory: _____

BUCKET LIST GOAL   Target Complete Date   Page #   Completed
_____   _____   _____   ☐
Partner A's Favorite Memory: _____
Partner B's Favorite Memory: _____

BUCKET LIST GOAL   Target Complete Date   Page #   Completed
_____   _____   _____   ☐
Partner A's Favorite Memory: _____
Partner B's Favorite Memory: _____

BUCKET LIST GOAL   Target Complete Date   Page #   Completed
_____   _____   _____   ☐
Partner A's Favorite Memory: _____
Partner B's Favorite Memory: _____

BUCKET LIST GOAL Target Complete Date Page # Completed

_____ _____ _____ ☐

Partner A's Favorite Memory: _____

Partner B's Favorite Memory: _____

BUCKET LIST GOAL Target Complete Date Page # Completed

_____ _____ _____ ☐

Partner A's Favorite Memory: _____

Partner B's Favorite Memory: _____

BUCKET LIST GOAL Target Complete Date Page # Completed

_____ _____ _____ ☐

Partner A's Favorite Memory: _____

Partner B's Favorite Memory: _____

BUCKET LIST GOAL Target Complete Date Page # Completed

_____ _____ _____ ☐

Partner A's Favorite Memory: _____

Partner B's Favorite Memory: _____

BUCKET LIST GOAL Target Complete Date Page # Completed

_____ _____ _____ ☐

Partner A's Favorite Memory: _____

Partner B's Favorite Memory: _____

BUCKET LIST GOAL Target Complete Date Page # Completed

_____ _____ _____ ☐

Partner A's Favorite Memory: _____

Partner B's Favorite Memory: _____

BUCKET LIST GOAL Target Complete Date Page # Completed

_____ _____ _____ ☐

Partner A's Favorite Memory: _____

Partner B's Favorite Memory: _____

BUCKET LIST GOAL   **Target Complete Date**   **Page #**   **Completed** ☐

Partner A's Favorite Memory: _____

Partner B's Favorite Memory: _____

BUCKET LIST GOAL   **Target Complete Date**   **Page #**   **Completed** ☐

Partner A's Favorite Memory: _____

Partner B's Favorite Memory: _____

BUCKET LIST GOAL   **Target Complete Date**   **Page #**   **Completed** ☐

Partner A's Favorite Memory: _____

Partner B's Favorite Memory: _____

BUCKET LIST GOAL   **Target Complete Date**   **Page #**   **Completed** ☐

Partner A's Favorite Memory: _____

Partner B's Favorite Memory: _____

BUCKET LIST GOAL   **Target Complete Date**   **Page #**   **Completed** ☐

Partner A's Favorite Memory: _____

Partner B's Favorite Memory: _____

BUCKET LIST GOAL   **Target Complete Date**   **Page #**   **Completed** ☐

Partner A's Favorite Memory: _____

Partner B's Favorite Memory: _____

BUCKET LIST GOAL   **Target Complete Date**   **Page #**   **Completed** ☐

Partner A's Favorite Memory: _____

Partner B's Favorite Memory: _____

BUCKET LIST GOAL   **Target Complete Date**   **Page #**   **Completed**

Partner A's Favorite Memory: _____

Partner B's Favorite Memory: _____

BUCKET LIST GOAL   **Target Complete Date**   **Page #**   **Completed**

Partner A's Favorite Memory: _____

Partner B's Favorite Memory: _____

BUCKET LIST GOAL   **Target Complete Date**   **Page #**   **Completed**

Partner A's Favorite Memory: _____

Partner B's Favorite Memory: _____

BUCKET LIST GOAL   **Target Complete Date**   **Page #**   **Completed**

Partner A's Favorite Memory: _____

Partner B's Favorite Memory: _____

BUCKET LIST GOAL   **Target Complete Date**   **Page #**   **Completed**

Partner A's Favorite Memory: _____

Partner B's Favorite Memory: _____

BUCKET LIST GOAL   **Target Complete Date**   **Page #**   **Completed**

Partner A's Favorite Memory: _____

Partner B's Favorite Memory: _____

BUCKET LIST GOAL   **Target Complete Date**   **Page #**   **Completed**

Partner A's Favorite Memory: _____

Partner B's Favorite Memory: _____

BUCKET LIST GOAL   Target Complete Date   Page #   Completed
_____   _____   _____   ☐

Partner A's Favorite Memory: _____
Partner B's Favorite Memory: _____

BUCKET LIST GOAL   Target Complete Date   Page #   Completed
_____   _____   _____   ☐

Partner A's Favorite Memory: _____
Partner B's Favorite Memory: _____

BUCKET LIST GOAL   Target Complete Date   Page #   Completed
_____   _____   _____   ☐

Partner A's Favorite Memory: _____
Partner B's Favorite Memory: _____

BUCKET LIST GOAL   Target Complete Date   Page #   Completed
_____   _____   _____   ☐

Partner A's Favorite Memory: _____
Partner B's Favorite Memory: _____

BUCKET LIST GOAL   Target Complete Date   Page #   Completed
_____   _____   _____   ☐

Partner A's Favorite Memory: _____
Partner B's Favorite Memory: _____

BUCKET LIST GOAL   Target Complete Date   Page #   Completed
_____   _____   _____   ☐

Partner A's Favorite Memory: _____
Partner B's Favorite Memory: _____

BUCKET LIST GOAL   Target Complete Date   Page #   Completed
_____   _____   _____   ☐

Partner A's Favorite Memory: _____
Partner B's Favorite Memory: _____

BUCKET LIST GOAL Target Complete Date Page # Completed

_____ _____ _____ ☐

Partner A's Favorite Memory: _____

Partner B's Favorite Memory: _____

BUCKET LIST GOAL Target Complete Date Page # Completed

_____ _____ _____ ☐

Partner A's Favorite Memory: _____

Partner B's Favorite Memory: _____

BUCKET LIST GOAL Target Complete Date Page # Completed

_____ _____ _____ ☐

Partner A's Favorite Memory: _____

Partner B's Favorite Memory: _____

BUCKET LIST GOAL Target Complete Date Page # Completed

_____ _____ _____ ☐

Partner A's Favorite Memory: _____

Partner B's Favorite Memory: _____

BUCKET LIST GOAL Target Complete Date Page # Completed

_____ _____ _____ ☐

Partner A's Favorite Memory: _____

Partner B's Favorite Memory: _____

BUCKET LIST GOAL Target Complete Date Page # Completed

_____ _____ _____ ☐

Partner A's Favorite Memory: _____

Partner B's Favorite Memory: _____

BUCKET LIST GOAL Target Complete Date Page # Completed

_____ _____ _____ ☐

Partner A's Favorite Memory: _____

Partner B's Favorite Memory: _____

BUCKET LIST GOAL   Target Complete Date   Page #   Completed
_____   _____   _____   ☐

Partner A's Favorite Memory: _____
Partner B's Favorite Memory: _____

BUCKET LIST GOAL   Target Complete Date   Page #   Completed
_____   _____   _____   ☐

Partner A's Favorite Memory: _____
Partner B's Favorite Memory: _____

BUCKET LIST GOAL   Target Complete Date   Page #   Completed
_____   _____   _____   ☐

Partner A's Favorite Memory: _____
Partner B's Favorite Memory: _____

BUCKET LIST GOAL   Target Complete Date   Page #   Completed
_____   _____   _____   ☐

Partner A's Favorite Memory: _____
Partner B's Favorite Memory: _____

BUCKET LIST GOAL   Target Complete Date   Page #   Completed
_____   _____   _____   ☐

Partner A's Favorite Memory: _____
Partner B's Favorite Memory: _____

BUCKET LIST GOAL   Target Complete Date   Page #   Completed
_____   _____   _____   ☐

Partner A's Favorite Memory: _____
Partner B's Favorite Memory: _____

BUCKET LIST GOAL   Target Complete Date   Page #   Completed
_____   _____   _____   ☐

Partner A's Favorite Memory: _____
Partner B's Favorite Memory: _____

BUCKET LIST GOAL   Target Complete Date   Page #   Completed
_____   _____   _____   ☐
_____

Partner A's Favorite Memory: _____

Partner B's Favorite Memory: _____

BUCKET LIST GOAL   Target Complete Date   Page #   Completed
_____   _____   _____   ☐
_____

Partner A's Favorite Memory: _____

Partner B's Favorite Memory: _____

BUCKET LIST GOAL   Target Complete Date   Page #   Completed
_____   _____   _____   ☐
_____

Partner A's Favorite Memory: _____

Partner B's Favorite Memory: _____

BUCKET LIST GOAL   Target Complete Date   Page #   Completed
_____   _____   _____   ☐
_____

Partner A's Favorite Memory: _____

Partner B's Favorite Memory: _____

BUCKET LIST GOAL   Target Complete Date   Page #   Completed
_____   _____   _____   ☐
_____

Partner A's Favorite Memory: _____

Partner B's Favorite Memory: _____

BUCKET LIST GOAL   Target Complete Date   Page #   Completed
_____   _____   _____   ☐
_____

Partner A's Favorite Memory: _____

Partner B's Favorite Memory: _____

BUCKET LIST GOAL   Target Complete Date   Page #   Completed
_____   _____   _____   ☐
_____

Partner A's Favorite Memory: _____

Partner B's Favorite Memory: _____

BUCKET LIST GOAL   **Target Complete Date**   **Page #**   **Completed**
⬜

_____   _____   _____

Partner A's Favorite Memory: _____

Partner B's Favorite Memory: _____

BUCKET LIST GOAL   **Target Complete Date**   **Page #**   **Completed**
⬜

_____   _____   _____

Partner A's Favorite Memory: _____

Partner B's Favorite Memory: _____

BUCKET LIST GOAL   **Target Complete Date**   **Page #**   **Completed**
⬜

_____   _____   _____

Partner A's Favorite Memory: _____

Partner B's Favorite Memory: _____

BUCKET LIST GOAL   **Target Complete Date**   **Page #**   **Completed**
⬜

_____   _____   _____

Partner A's Favorite Memory: _____

Partner B's Favorite Memory: _____

BUCKET LIST GOAL   **Target Complete Date**   **Page #**   **Completed**
⬜

_____   _____   _____

Partner A's Favorite Memory: _____

Partner B's Favorite Memory: _____

BUCKET LIST GOAL   **Target Complete Date**   **Page #**   **Completed**
⬜

_____   _____   _____

Partner A's Favorite Memory: _____

Partner B's Favorite Memory: _____

BUCKET LIST GOAL   **Target Complete Date**   **Page #**   **Completed**
⬜

_____   _____   _____

Partner A's Favorite Memory: _____

Partner B's Favorite Memory: _____

Resources

Online

Dr. Wyatt Fisher, DrWyattFisher.com
Learn more about the Total Marriage Refresh seminars that are conducted across the country.

HerSideHisSide, HerSideHisSide.com
A relationship and dating website that gives advice from both a masculine and a feminine perspective.

Inspiyr, Inspiyr.com
Provides articles related to motivation, success, and self-improvement.

Lifehack, Lifehack.org
Covers a variety of topics including relationships, communication, and self-improvement.

LovePanky, LovePanky.com
Gives a wide range of relationship advice, from romantic to adventurous.

Relationship Development and Transformation Magazine, Relationship-Development.com
A great resource for all kinds of dating and relationship advice.

Books

Couple's Bucket List: 101 Fun, Engaging Dating Ideas by Dr. Carol Morgan
Provides unique date ideas for couples to create lifelong memories and strengthen their connection.

The Ultimate Relationship Workbook for Couples: Simple Exercises to Improve Communication and Strengthen Your Bond by Dr. Ari Sytner, LCSW, MEd
Offers a simple but comprehensive exploration of your romantic partnership.

The Couple's Activity Book: 70 Interactive Games to Strengthen Your Relationship by Crystal Schwanke
Helps couples build a stronger bond with playful, interactive games and activities.

A Year of Us: A Couple's Journal: One Question a Day to Spark Fun and Meaningful Conversation by Alicia Muñoz, LPC
Provides a year's worth of engaging prompts to help couples explore important aspects of their relationship.

The Couple's Quiz Book: 350 Fun Questions to Energize Your Relationship by Alicia Muñoz, LPC
Find fun quizzes for couples to grow their relationship.

Index

About the Author

DR. CAROL MORGAN, PhD, is a relationship, dating, and success expert and a professor at Wright State University. She earned her PhD in gender and interpersonal communication from the University of Nebraska.

In addition to teaching, she is a relationship and dating coach, conducts Total Marriage Refresh seminars for married couples, and is the host of the *E-Love with Dr. Carol* radio show.

She is the author of several books, including *Couple's Bucket List: 101 Fun, Engaging Dating Ideas*. She has also written hundreds of articles and appeared in videos for many popular websites such as the *Huffington Post*, LovePanky, Lifehack, and eHow. Her articles have been shared on social media millions of times.

Dr. Carol regularly appears as an expert on the TV show *Living Dayton* to share relationship and motivational advice. In addition, she has been a featured expert on DatingAdvice.com, Relationship-Development.com, and Inspiyr.com. She is also the founder of HerSideHisSide.com, where she provides advice on dating and relationships.

She has two grown sons, Colton and Chase, and lives in Dayton, Ohio, with her husband, Joe.

You can reach Dr. Carol through her websites: HerSideHisSide.com and DrCarolMorgan.com.